THE NUMERICAL AND TIME CORRELATIONS IN THE QURAN

Sahal A. Mohamed

 FriesenPress

Suite 300 - 990 Fort St
Victoria, BC, V8V 3K2
Canada

www.friesenpress.com

Copyright © 2018 by Sahal A. Mohamed
First Edition — 2018

All rights reserved.

No part of this publication may be reproduced in any form, or by any means, electronic or mechanical, including photocopying, recording, or any information browsing, storage, or retrieval system, without permission in writing from FriesenPress.

ISBN
978-1-5255-3002-9 (Hardcover)
978-1-5255-3003-6 (Paperback)
978-1-5255-3004-3 (eBook)

1. RELIGION, ISLAM, KORAN & SACRED WRITINGS

Distributed to the trade by The Ingram Book Company

TABLE OF CONTENTS

XI
PROLOGUE

1
CHAPTER 1
The Daily Prayers And Ramadan

7
CHAPTER 2
The Quran's Interactions With Time

24
CHAPTER 3
Calendars In The Quran

28
CHAPTER 4
The Quran Numbers Conformity With The Time

45
CHAPTER 5
The Relationship Between Time And The Quran's Conservation

54
CHAPTER 6
Harmony Between Faith And The Time

69
CHAPTER 7
How Time Is Complementary To Human Creation

86
CHAPTER 8
The Creation Of Jesus

102
CHAPTER 9
Miscellaneous Verses Relevant To Time

To my father
ABDI M. NUUR DACAR
and my mother
ANAB OSMAN "Qalanbac"

This book would not have been possible without the support of **Abdinasir J. Yusuf**, who helped me by typing, drawing models, and formatting tables. I am so grateful for his valuable time and unlimited suggestions.

To my son, Guled Sahal, who helped me with the counting and calculations of the Quran's words and letters.

I am so grateful to Richard Counsil, a librarian at the Seattle Public Library, who gave me so much help with writing and researching.

Finally, I am very delightful the unlimited support from my wife Qani Mohamed.

PROLOGUE

Muslims consider the Quran a holy book and the precise word of Allah. The Quran is quite different from other Arabic poetry and doesn't conform to the standards commonly used in the written and spoken language. Muslims claim that the Quran is beyond human capability and is therefore attributed to the divine. When I started this research, which took me more than six years, I began to look at the Quran from a different perspective. I became fascinated with how it expresses time and other important numerical concepts. I don't mean time as Newton, Galileo, Einstein, or Hawking would express it, because that is a rather fluid topic. Instead, I will discuss how the Quran defines the fundamentals of time by looking at how the actual words in the text connect with one another.

I began my research to explore several questions: Why is the Quran primarily composed of two sections, Makki and Madani? Why is it divided into thirty chapters, sixty sub-chapters, and seven stages? If you look at a standard copy of the Quran, you will notice that most pages are composed of fifteen lines, with each opposite page containing thirty lines. It may seem like this was accidental, but why do these numbers align with the division of time in our calendars? Why do most verses that deal with the concept of time correlate with common time-related numbers? Why does Allah claim He is time? Why is the Quran so enigmatic regarding time?

Why does the Quran mention the duration of Ramadan, the Haj, and inheritance accurately, but does not remind us when and how many times per day we should pray? Prayer is the backbone of our religion and we are instructed about it directly by Allah through his Messenger. Why, then, does the Quran not mention how many elements (*rakats**) are in our prayers (*salah*[*1])? I have contemplated these difficult questions for several years.

Are the answers to these questions found in the Quran? One would think it would be explained with detail. I will discuss that at length in the following chapters. We Muslims claim that the Quran doesn't mention the number of daily prayers, but I will prove the answer has been there all along. I will also discuss the miracles in the Quran relating to time. The correlations, I argue, are not accidental. What I have discovered will surprise both Muslims and non-Muslims.

I believe that if the Quran talks about time, it must mathematically align with all time-related numbers, without exception. I decided to put this hypothesis to the test. I first investigated whether my expectations were on track or not. I went deep into the Quran to prove that it does not contradict itself mathematically. After I arrived at the precise time-related numbers, I predicted that more and more verses, page numbers, surahs, and chapters would fall in with my expectations. As I examined many verses, I had my 'Aha' moment!

---

1   *Some Arabic words are spelled differently when written in English*

Allah, through His Messenger, said, "Sons of Adam insult against the time, and I am time, in My hand is the night and the day." This was related by al-Bukhari. In my young years, anytime I listened to this hadith, I was buzzed. Why does God confirm that He is time? I guessed that the answer would reveal the secrets behind why time-related numbers continuously emerge through patterns in His words whenever time is mentioned. It would be ridiculous to align everything in the Quran with time, but I was shocked how many surahs, verses, page numbers, and so on seem to conform to measurements of time. I didn't run a special word counting program for this research; I simply used my pencil, note book, and calculator.

Some Islamic scholars or readers will question my approach or my unorthodox explanations, but those challenges are part of life and I look forward to viewing the Quran in a new light every time I read it. I can perceive it in my own way without being distracted by its authenticity. I highly respect the old scholars' opinions and their concepts in interpreting the Quran, as well as their noble contributions in the service of Islam.

I decided to simplify this analysis using basic language and math to make it comprehensible to all readers. In my application of mathematics, I use the numbers as they fit the results. Skeptics may argue that I am trying to force the mathematical solutions to fit what I would like them to be; however, I am not the first one to use this approach. Many people have written about certain numbers in the Quran, but their approaches have been limited. Humans have always used mathematics to describe a situation. R.W. Hamming wrote, "To assert that the world can be explained via mathematics amounts to an act of faith."[2] Sometimes in math, the result you expect is explained by how you got there. Wigner sums up his argument by saying, "The enormous usefulness of mathematics in the natural sciences is something bordering on the mysterious and there is no rational explanation for it."[3] Add, subtract, divide, and multiply—the time-related numbers are ready to be explored from verse to verse and from chapter to chapter.

After I went deeply into some verses in the Quran, I recognized that these are not human words, but are instead much nobler. They could not have come from an illiterate man living in a remote desert region, only from the Almighty Lord.

Although I spent many years, from the age of eight, sitting in front of Somali Quran interpreters, I later exercised my Arabic knowledge to study other opinions from Muslim scholars. With that, I decided to review the Quran in a distinctive way. Throughout this work, I use basic mathematics like addition and square roots to relate the numbers of the Quran to common numbers used in the division of time. These include twelve, representing the hours of the day and night and the months of the year, seven for the days of the week, and sixty for the seconds in a minute and minutes of an hour."

It was a challenging task to study while living through civil war and being a refugee. I did not choose this situation, and I

---

2   Hamming, R. W. (1980). "The Unreasonable Effectiveness of Mathematics". The American Mathematical Monthly. 87 (2): Quoting in Eugene Wigner's paper, "The Unreasonable Effectiveness of Mathematics in the Natural Sciences".

3   "The unreasonable effectiveness of mathematics in the natural sciences". Richard Courant lecture in mathematical sciences delivered at New York University, May 11, 1959.

experienced the terrible physical and psychological pain that comes with killing and destruction. I decided to review only certain parts or surahs to accomplish my project, and they are a small portion of the Quran. However, they will reveal secrets and codes buried deeply in the holy book, and I look forward to pursuing more research when I get to a safe and secure country.

CHAPTER 1
THE DAILY PRAYERS AND RAMADAN

Don't use any papers that contain numbers in the restrooms, because numbers are blessed by God.

—Somali wisdom

THE DAILY PRAYERS

In every part of the Islamic religion, preachers and scholars maintain that the number of daily prayers (five) and the number of elements (*rakah*s) in the prayers (seventeen) are never mentioned in the Quran. Instead, it is instruction from the Prophet Muhammad (SAW). Let's examine this argument.

Why does the Quran mention Ramadan, the pilgrimage, the process of divorce, and even ablutions, but the most vital part of Islam, which is praying five times a day, is never mentioned?

According to the Quran, Allah orders us to pray to Him but doesn't mention how many times a day. If the holy book talks about these arbitrary things, then why doesn't it go into full detail about daily prayers?

Does the Quran demonstrate in some other way how many times we should pray? Did Allah put this in code somewhere? I believe He did, and I will demonstrate it mathematically.

The numerical and time correlations in the Quran

Looking at Al-Baqarah verses 144, 149, and 150, it is clear that these lines were revealed after the permanent change of direction (*qiblah*) toward Makkah for all Muslim prayers. Muslims were praying toward Jerusalem and towards Mecca was added later.

قَدْ نَرَىٰ تَقَلُّبَ وَجْهِكَ فِى ٱلسَّمَاءِ ۖ فَلَنُوَلِّيَنَّكَ قِبْلَةً تَرْضَىٰهَا ۚ فَوَلِّ وَجْهَكَ شَطْرَ ٱلْمَسْجِدِ ٱلْحَرَامِ ۚ وَحَيْثُ مَا كُنتُمْ فَوَلُّوا۟ وُجُوهَكُمْ شَطْرَهُۥ ۗ وَإِنَّ ٱلَّذِينَ أُوتُوا۟ ٱلْكِتَٰبَ لَيَعْلَمُونَ أَنَّهُ ٱلْحَقُّ مِن رَّبِّهِمْ ۗ وَمَا ٱللَّهُ بِغَٰفِلٍ عَمَّا يَعْمَلُونَ (١٤٤)

We see the turning of thy face (for guidance) to the heavens; now shall We turn thee to a Qiblah that shall please thee. Turn then thy face in the direction of the Sacred Mosque; wherever ye are turn your faces in that direction. The people of the book know well that that is the truth from their Lord nor is Allah unmindful of what they do. (144)

This verse number is 144, which is the square of number 12. Twelve represents the hours of day or night, and the months of both lunar and solar years.

وَمِنْ حَيْثُ خَرَجْتَ فَوَلِّ وَجْهَكَ شَطْرَ ٱلْمَسْجِدِ ٱلْحَرَامِ ۖ وَإِنَّهُ لَلْحَقُّ مِن رَّبِّكَ ۗ وَمَا ٱللَّهُ بِغَٰفِلٍ عَمَّا تَعْمَلُونَ (١٤٩)

From whencesoever thou startest forth, turn thy face in the direction of the Sacred Mosque; that is indeed the truth from thy Lord. And Allah is not unmindful of what ye do. (149)

وَمِنْ حَيْثُ خَرَجْتَ فَوَلِّ وَجْهَكَ شَطْرَ ٱلْمَسْجِدِ ٱلْحَرَامِ ۚ وَحَيْثُ مَا كُنتُمْ فَوَلُّوا۟ وُجُوهَكُمْ شَطْرَهُۥ لِئَلَّا يَكُونَ لِلنَّاسِ عَلَيْكُمْ حُجَّةٌ إِلَّا ٱلَّذِينَ ظَلَمُوا۟ مِنْهُمْ فَلَا تَخْشَوْهُمْ وَٱخْشَوْنِى وَلِأُتِمَّ نِعْمَتِى عَلَيْكُمْ وَلَعَلَّكُمْ تَهْتَدُونَ (١٥٠)

So, from whencesoever thou startest forth turn thy face in the direction of the Sacred Mosque; and wheresoever ye are turn your face thither That there be no ground of dispute

against you among the people Except those of them that are bent on wickedness; so fear them not but fear Me; and that I may complete My favors on you and ye may (consent to) be guided. (150)

Table 1

شَطْرَ	وَجْهَكَ	فَوَلٌّ
شَطْرَ	وَجْهَكَ	فَوَلٌّ
شَطْرَ	وَجْهَكَ	فَوَلٌّ
شَطْرَهُ	وُجُوهَكُمْ	فَوَلُّواْ
شَطْرَهُ	وُجُوهَكُمْ	فَوَلُّواْ

Total letters	17	24	17

وُجُوهَكُمْ (wujuuhakum and wajhaka) are mentioned five times and have a total of twenty-four letters, which reflects the hours in a full day. The total letters at the table above also show these three words are repeated five times in these three verses. This may refer to the five daily prayers. If you add all letters of فَوَلٌّ, شَطْرَهُ, شَطْرَ, and فَوَلُّواْ and omit the additional *alif*, the total is seventeen, which suggests the number of elements (*rakahs*) in a day. Furthermore, Allah indicates the timeframe using the words وَجْهَكَ (wajhaka and wujuuhakum) in twenty-four, which reinforces the idea behind the number of daily *rakahs* in the twenty-four hours of a day. These mathematical correlations could not appear by accident.

Why does Allah use these three words exactly five times? I argue that the directive to give five daily prayers is encoded in these verses.

An-Nissa (The Women)

(إِنَّ ٱلصَّلَوٰةَ كَانَتْ عَلَى ٱلْمُؤْمِنِينَ كِتَـٰبًا مَّوْقُوتًا ١٠٣)

Worship at fixed times hath been enjoined on the believers. (103)

This verse contains seven words. Scheduled daily prayers are required throughout the week, with some exceptions. The alignment of seven days with seven characters wouldn't be a coincidence. The call to prayer comes at specific times of the day, and Muslims are expected to follow each instance."

RAMADAN

Ramadan is a one-month tradition practiced by all Muslims. It normally covers 29-30 days; therefore, we should have evidence in the Quran that the fasting period would be that length. In the Quran, Allah mentions that Ramadan is only one month. This is known, but I will prove it mathematically using the holy text.

Whether we fast for twenty-nine or thirty days depends on the length of the lunar month. Let us do simple mathematics using the Quran to reveal evidence of both twenty-nine and thirty days.

Al-Baqarah (The Cow)

يَـٰٓأَيُّهَا ٱلَّذِينَ ءَامَنُوا۟ كُتِبَ عَلَيْكُمُ ٱلصِّيَامُ كَمَا كُتِبَ عَلَى ٱلَّذِينَ مِن قَبْلِكُمْ
(لَعَلَّكُمْ تَتَّقُونَ ١٨٣)

O ye who believe! fasting is prescribed to you as it was prescribed to those before you that ye may (learn) self-restraint. (183)

أَيَّامًا مَّعْدُودَاتٍ ۚ فَمَن كَانَ مِنكُم مَّرِيضًا أَوْ عَلَىٰ سَفَرٍ فَعِدَّةٌ مِّنْ أَيَّامٍ أُخَرَ ۚ وَعَلَى ٱلَّذِينَ يُطِيقُونَهُۥ فِدْيَةٌ طَعَامُ مِسْكِينٍ ۖ فَمَن تَطَوَّعَ خَيْرًا فَهُوَ خَيْرٌ لَّهُۥ ۚ وَأَن (تَصُومُواْ) خَيْرٌ لَّكُمْ ۖ إِن كُنتُمْ تَعْلَمُونَ (١٨٤)

(Fasting) for a fixed number of days; but if any of you is ill or on a journey, the prescribed number (should be made up) from days later. For those who can do it (with hardship) is a ransom, the feeding of one that is indigent. But he that will give more of his own free-will—it is better for him, and it is better for you that ye fast, if ye only knew. (184)

شَهْرُ رَمَضَانَ ٱلَّذِىٓ أُنزِلَ فِيهِ ٱلْقُرْءَانُ هُدًى لِّلنَّاسِ وَبَيِّنَٰتٍ مِّنَ ٱلْهُدَىٰ وَٱلْفُرْقَانِ ۚ فَمَن شَهِدَ مِنكُمُ ٱلشَّهْرَ فَلْيَصُمْهُ ۖ وَمَن كَانَ مَرِيضًا أَوْ عَلَىٰ سَفَرٍ فَعِدَّةٌ مِّنْ أَيَّامٍ أُخَرَ ۗ يُرِيدُ ٱللَّهُ بِكُمُ ٱلْيُسْرَ وَلَا يُرِيدُ بِكُمُ ٱلْعُسْرَ وَلِتُكْمِلُواْ ٱلْعِدَّةَ (وَلِتُكَبِّرُواْ) ٱللَّهَ عَلَىٰ مَا هَدَىٰكُمْ وَلَعَلَّكُمْ تَشْكُرُونَ (١٨٥)

Ramadan is the (month) in which was sent down the Quran as a guide to mankind also clear (Signs) for guidance and judgment (between right and wrong). So, every one of you who is present (at his home) during that month should spend it in fasting, but if anyone is ill, or on a journey, the prescribed period (should be made up) by days later. Allah intends every facility for you He does not want to put you to difficulties. (He wants you) to complete the prescribed period, and to glorify Him in that He has guided you; and perchance ye shall be grateful. (185)

The numerical and time correlations in the Quran

أُحِلَّ لَكُمْ لَيْلَةَ **ٱلصِّيَامِ** ٱلرَّفَثُ إِلَىٰ نِسَآئِكُمْ ۚ هُنَّ لِبَاسٌ لَّكُمْ وَأَنتُمْ لِبَاسٌ لَّهُنَّ ۗ عَلِمَ ٱللَّهُ أَنَّكُمْ كُنتُمْ تَخْتَانُونَ أَنفُسَكُمْ فَتَابَ عَلَيْكُمْ وَعَفَا عَنكُمْ ۖ فَٱلْـَٰٔنَ بَـٰشِرُوهُنَّ وَٱبْتَغُوا۟ مَا كَتَبَ ٱللَّهُ لَكُمْ ۚ وَكُلُوا۟ وَٱشْرَبُوا۟ حَتَّىٰ يَتَبَيَّنَ لَكُمُ ٱلْخَيْطُ ٱلْأَبْيَضُ مِنَ ٱلْخَيْطِ ٱلْأَسْوَدِ مِنَ ٱلْفَجْرِ ۖ ثُمَّ أَتِمُّوا۟ **ٱلصِّيَامَ** إِلَى ٱلَّيْلِ ۚ وَلَا تُبَـٰشِرُوهُنَّ وَأَنتُمْ عَـٰكِفُونَ فِى ٱلْمَسَـٰجِدِ ۗ تِلْكَ حُدُودُ ٱللَّهِ فَلَا تَقْرَبُوهَا ۗ كَذَٰلِكَ يُبَيِّنُ ٱللَّهُ ءَايَـٰتِهِۦ لِلنَّاسِ لَعَلَّهُمْ يَتَّقُونَ (١٨٧)

Permitted to you on the night of the fasts, is the approach to your wives. They are your garments. And ye are their garments. Allah know what ye used to do secretly among yourselves; but He turned to you and forgave you; so now associate with them, and seek what Allah hath ordained for you and eat and drink, until the white thread of dawn appear to you distinct from its black thread; then complete your fast till the night appears; but do not associate with your wives while ye are in retreat in the mosques. Those are limits (set by) Allah; approach not nigh thereto. Thus, doth Allah make clear His signs to men that they may learn self-restraint. (187)

The underlined and bolded word for fast (*siyyam*) is five words, each containing six letters; 6 x 5 = 30. This represents the number of days we fast. If we omit the additional *alif*, the result will be ([6 x 5] -1) = 29. The meaning of ٱلصِّيَام is fasting, which is fascinating because even though Allah doesn't state the number of days to fast, He shows us through the miraculous numerical correlations.

CHAPTER 2
THE QURAN'S INTERACTIONS WITH TIME

Arithmetic is numbers you squeeze from your head to your hand to your pencil to your paper until you get the answer.

~ Carl Sandburg, «Arithmetic»

I found strong correlations between the number of surahs in the Quran and the number twelve. Why do these correlations exist? Twelve is the root of 144. If this is subtracted from 114, which is the number of surahs in the Quran, it gives thirty—the days of one month, whether lunar or solar.

Time is measured in seconds, minutes, hours, days, weeks, months, years, and centuries. Each day and night consist of twelve hours, totaling twenty-four. There are seven days in the week. Depending on the month, there are twenty-nine, thirty, or thirty-one days. Twelve months complete the yearly cycle.

Depending on the version and interpretation, there are either 6226 or 6236 verses in the Quran. You will be stunned at how these numbers align with time. If you split the number in half, you get 62 and 26. If you multiply the digits in both numbers, 6 and 2, you get 12. Multiplying the 6 with 2 and adding 6 by 2, the result is 24—the hours of a full day. The other version is correlated to time too. Split it as 6, 2, and 36. Six by 2 is 12, but 36 is directly related to time as well. Multiply 6 and 2 to get 12, and 3 with 6 to get 18. Added together, the sum is 30—the number of days in a month. There are also twelve surahs that have time-related names.

Is this an accident? Why do humans choose to use dozens in many businesses? Do they prefer the number twelve by accident, or is this number the first they learned to use that is suitable for their daily dealings?

I was amazed when I landed in Seattle and everyone was wearing fluorescent green and dark blue T-shirts, hats, and more showing the number twelve. Seattle Seahawks' fans use number twelve. Why the intense love for this number? Even I received a gift—a hat tailored with the lovely time-related number twelve! I liked it and it conforms to my expectations of time and the Quran.

The following calculations are based on working with Arabic words and their letters in this beautiful language chosen by Allah.

Table 2

Name of surah	Meaning
Al-Israa	The Night Journey
An-Najm	The Star
Al-Qamar	The Moon
Al-Jumah	Friday
Al-Qiyamah	The Day of Resurrection
Al-Fajr	The Dawn

The Quran's Interactions With Time

Attariq	The Morning Star
Ash-shams	The Sun
Al-Layl	The Night
Ad-Duha	The Morning
Al-Asr	The Era
Al-Falaq	The Day Break

There are twenty-nine surahs that contain *alif laam meem, nuun, qaaf, alif laam miim ra, alif laam meem saad, xaa meem*, and so on. As seen in table 2 above, there are exactly twelve suras that are named a time-related name.

The ratio (29/114) of these surahs combined (*alif laam meem, noon, qaaf etc.*) of the total Quran, are 0.25438 Multiplying this by 1000, the product is 254.38. Add this to 100 to get 354.38, which is exactly the number days of the lunar year. Surprisingly, 1000 and 100 are also contained in the Quran. In surah Al-Baqarah verse 96, it mentions 1000 years of living. In verse 259, one of the Israeli prophets reaches a ruined village and asks, "How will Allah bring this to life after its death?" Allah made him dead a hundred years. Why did God need these numbers in the Quran? Why does Allah adopt those and other time-related numbers in most verses that specify time? On the other hand, what if these time-related numbers occur only by coincidence?

Let us use simple probability.

What is the chance of getting one verse that precisely describes something about time?

1/6226=0.000160616768392

What are the chances that there is a second verse that also mentions time?

The probability could always be zero.

1/6226 x 1/6226 = 0.000000025797746

The Quran contains more than 77,000 words and 320,000 letters. The chance of one word in the correct place should be 0.00001299. What are the chances of a second word, third, fourth, and so on? And the chance of one letter?

No one can dispute the numbers because there is no fault in math. The chance of having a complete verse or sentence that coincidentally describes time-related numbers is zero. Could any mathematician claim that the Quran was written by chance?

There is no coincidence in the calculations made by God. He is the One, He revealed the Quran, and He was attentive and mindful of what He was talking about. He has complete knowledge of mathematics and calibrations, as cited in His Holy Books.

In this surah, Allah specifies precisely that a year is strictly twelve months, whether it is lunar or solar.

This is my favorite verse and I inspired by what I discovered about time within it. My jaw dropped when I counted and calculated this mathematically. It was awesome. My heart was beating strangely, and I felt the power of the Quran. My feelings were very unusual.

Let's analyze the parts of surah *Al-Tawba* and my favorite verse, number thirty-six.

Al-Tawba (The Repentance)

إِنَّ عِدَّةَ ٱلشُّهُورِ عِندَ ٱللَّهِ ٱثْنَا عَشَرَ شَهْرًا

فِى كِتَٰبِ ٱللَّهِ يَوْمَ خَلَقَ ٱلسَّمَٰوَٰتِ وَٱلْأَرْضَ

مِنْهَآ أَرْبَعَةٌ حُرُمٌ

ذَٰلِكَ ٱلدِّينُ ٱلْقَيِّمُ فَلَا تَظْلِمُوا۟ فِيهِنَّ أَنفُسَكُمْ

The first part of the verse has exactly twenty-nine letters, which refers to the number of days in a month in the lunar calendar. The second part of the verse contains thirty letters, which indicates the number of lunar or solar days in a month. The third part of the verse is made up of twelve letters, which represents the months of a year. The last part of the verse shows seven words for the number of days in a week. What is this perfection? It can't be a coincidence that Allah would talk about time and have the numbers in the text reflect that. This conformity can't be expressed by any human being. It is a supernatural marvel.

Now let's delve deeper into surah *Al-Tawba*. It mentions the word Allah 169 times, at least once on each page. Let's analyze the two pages that contain the fewest numbers of Allah—pages 9 and 21. If you subtract 21 from 9, the outcome is 12.

Three pages in surah *Al-Tawba* mention the word Allah seven times. In addition, three pages in the surah mention the word Allah eight times. If we multiply 7 by 3, we get 21. If we multiply 8 by 3, we get 24.

7 x 3 = 21
8 x 3 = 24
7+8 = 15
21+24 = 45
45 +15 = 60

You might be guessing what sixty means already, and you're probably right: this represents either sixty minutes in an hour or sixty seconds in a minute.

Verse 80

(ذَٰلِكَ بِأَنَّهُمْ كَفَرُوا۟ بِٱللَّهِ وَرَسُولِهِۦ ۗ وَٱللَّهُ لَا يَهْدِى ٱلْقَوْمَ ٱلْفَٰسِقِينَ ٨٠) ٱسْتَغْفِرْ لَهُمْ أَوْ لَا تَسْتَغْفِرْ لَهُمْ إِن تَسْتَغْفِرْ لَهُمْ سَبْعِينَ مَرَّةً فَلَن يَغْفِرَ ٱللَّهُ لَهُمْ

Whether thou ask for their forgiveness or not, (their sin is unforgivable): if thou ask seventy times for their forgiveness, Allah will not forgive them: because they have rejected Allah and His Messenger; and Allah guideth not those who are perversely rebellious. (80)

This verse has twenty-seven words and 103 letters. In this verse, Allah is mentioned seventy times. Let us play with these numbers to relate them to time.

If you add up the numbers, you get 210. If you subtract the total from the days of the lunar year (354), the result is 144. The root of 144 is 12. On the other hand, if you add 20, 80, and 27, your result will be 177, which is half of the lunar year.

80+103+27=210
354-210=144
√144=12
70+80+27=177

Verse 118

وَعَلَى ٱلثَّلَٰثَةِ ٱلَّذِينَ خُلِّفُوا۟ حَتَّىٰٓ إِذَا ضَاقَتْ عَلَيْهِمُ ٱلْأَرْضُ بِمَا رَحُبَتْ وَضَاقَتْ عَلَيْهِمْ أَنفُسُهُمْ وَظَنُّوٓا۟ أَن لَّا مَلْجَأَ مِنَ ٱللَّهِ إِلَّآ إِلَيْهِ ثُمَّ تَابَ عَلَيْهِمْ لِيَتُوبُوٓا۟ إِنَّ ٱللَّهَ هُوَ ٱلتَّوَّابُ ٱلرَّحِيمُ (١١٨)

(He turned in mercy also) to the three who were left behind: (they felt guilty) to such a degree that the earth seemed constrained to them, for all its spaciousness and their (very) souls seemed straitened to them— and they perceived that there is no fleeing from Allah (and no refuge) but to Himself. Then He turned to them, that they might repent: for Allah is Oft-Returning, Most Merciful. (118)

In this verse, Allah addresses three people. Multiplying three with 118 (the number of the verse), the result is 354, the days of the lunar year.

Finally, the stunner is that surah *Al-Tawba* has 129 verses in total. Add these numbers together (1+2+9) to get twelve!

No human being could arrange these words with this perfection.

AL-FATIHAH (THE OPENING)

بِسْمِ ٱللَّهِ ٱلرَّحْمَٰنِ ٱلرَّحِيمِ (١) ٱلْحَمْدُ لِلَّهِ رَبِّ ٱلْعَٰلَمِينَ (٢) ٱلرَّحْمَٰنِ ٱلرَّحِيمِ (٣) مَٰلِكِ يَوْمِ ٱلدِّينِ (٤) إِيَّاكَ نَعْبُدُ وَإِيَّاكَ نَسْتَعِينُ (٥) ٱهْدِنَا ٱلصِّرَٰطَ ٱلْمُسْتَقِيمَ (٦) صِرَٰطَ ٱلَّذِينَ أَنْعَمْتَ عَلَيْهِمْ غَيْرِ ٱلْمَغْضُوبِ عَلَيْهِمْ وَلَا ٱلضَّآلِّينَ (٧)

The numerical and time correlations in the Quran

In the name of Allah, the Beneficent, the Merciful (1) Praise be to Allah, Lord of the Worlds, (2) The Beneficent, the Merciful. (3) Owner of the Day of Judgment, (4) Thee (alone) we worship; Thee (alone) we ask for help. (5) Show us the straight path, (6) The path of those whom Thou hast favoured. Not (the path) of those who earn Thine anger nor of those who go astray. (7)

Al-Fatiha (The Opener) is the most monumental surah in the Quran. Why does it have only seven verses? It is uttered dozens of times a day. Depending on how you read the surah, it consists of either 144 letters if it's Maliki (ملك), or 145 if it's Maaliki (مَالِك).

The verses of *Al-Fatiha* contain the following number of letters: 13, 20, 18, **12**, 19, 19, 44. Look where number twelve is located! It hooks at the heart of the surah (the mean). Is it coded accidentally or there is wisdom behind that? Another amazing miracle is the placement of the word *yawm* (day) in the highlighted word. It is found in the twelfth position in the surah.

If you multiply the greatest and the least numbers (13 and 44), you get 528. If you subtract the sum of all the numbers from the product of the previous equation, you get 384. Then you subtract the mode (nineteen) from the product of the sum. The result is 365, the days of the solar year. Then subtract 384 by 30 (18+12) to get 354, which is the number of days in the lunar calendar year.

Lastly, if you multiply the maximum by thirteen, you get 572. Its square is 23.9, which is basically 24. This represents the hours in a day.

13 + 20 + 18 + 12 + 19 + 19 + 44 = 144
44 x 12 = 528
528 - 144 = 384
384 - 19 = 365
384 - 30 = 354
13 x 44 = 572
√572=23.9≈24
√144=12

Al-Baqarah

Ayat Al-Kursi (The Throne verse)

اَللَّهُ لَا إِلَٰهَ إِلَّا هُوَ ٱلْحَىُّ ٱلْقَيُّومُ لَا تَأْخُذُهُ سِنَةٌ وَلَا نَوْمٌ لَّهُ مَا فِى ٱلسَّمَٰوَٰتِ وَمَا فِى ٱلْأَرْضِ مَن ذَا ٱلَّذِى يَشْفَعُ عِندَهُ إِلَّا بِإِذْنِهِ يَعْلَمُ مَا بَيْنَ أَيْدِيهِمْ وَمَا خَلْفَهُمْ وَلَا يُحِيطُونَ بِشَىْءٍ مِّنْ عِلْمِهِ إِلَّا بِمَا شَآءَ وَسِعَ كُرْسِيُّهُ ٱلسَّمَٰوَٰتِ وَٱلْأَرْضَ وَلَا يَـُٔودُهُ حِفْظُهُمَا وَهُوَ ٱلْعَلِىُّ ٱلْعَظِيمُ (٢٥٥)

Allah! There is no God save Him, the Alive, the Eternal. Neither slumber nor sleep overtakes Him. Unto Him belongeth whatsoever is in the heavens and whatsoever is in the earth. Who is he that intercedes with Him save by His leave? He knoweth that which is in front of them and that which is behind them, while they encompass nothing of His knowledge save what He will. His throne included the heavens and the earth, and He is never weary of preserving them. He is the Sublime, the Tremendous. (255)

This is an enormous verse in the Quran and its number is 255. If the numbers are separated and added up, the sum is twelve. This verse contains fifty-seven words and adding those two numbers together is also twelve. The page number of the verse is forty-two. The sum of 255, 57, and 42 is 354, the days of the lunar year. What are the secrets behind this?

2+5+5=12
5+7=12
255+57+42=354

Verse 259

أَوْ كَالَّذِى مَرَّ عَلَىٰ قَرْيَةٍ وَهِىَ خَاوِيَةٌ عَلَىٰ عُرُوشِهَا قَالَ أَنَّىٰ يُحْىِۦ هَـٰذِهِ ٱللَّهُ بَعْدَ مَوْتِهَا ۖ فَأَمَاتَهُ ٱللَّهُ مِا۟ئَةَ عَامٍ ثُمَّ بَعَثَهُۥ ۖ قَالَ كَمْ لَبِثْتَ ۖ قَالَ لَبِثْتُ يَوْمًا أَوْ بَعْضَ يَوْمٍ ۖ قَالَ بَل لَّبِثْتَ مِا۟ئَةَ عَامٍ فَٱنظُرْ إِلَىٰ طَعَامِكَ وَشَرَابِكَ لَمْ يَتَسَنَّهْ ۖ وَٱنظُرْ إِلَىٰ حِمَارِكَ وَلِنَجْعَلَكَ ءَايَةً لِّلنَّاسِ ۖ وَٱنظُرْ إِلَى ٱلْعِظَامِ كَيْفَ نُنشِزُهَا ثُمَّ نَكْسُوهَا لَحْمًا ۚ فَلَمَّا تَبَيَّنَ لَهُۥ قَالَ أَعْلَمُ أَنَّ ٱللَّهَ عَلَىٰ كُلِّ شَىْءٍ قَدِيرٌ (٢٥٩)

Or (bethink thee of) the like of him who, passing by a township which had fallen into utter ruin, exclaimed: How shall Allah give this township life after its death? And Allah made him die a hundred years, then brought him back to life. He said: How long hast thou tarried? (The man) said: I have tarried a day or part of a day. (He) said: Nay, but thou hast tarried for a hundred years. Just look at thy food and drink which have not rotted! Look at thine ass! And, that We may make thee a token unto mankind, look at the bones, how We adjust them and then cover them with flesh! And when (the matter) became clear unto him, he said: I know now that Allah is Able to do all things. (259)

This verse describes how one of the prophets died in a hundred years and then Allah brought him to life.

This verse is on page 43 and contains seventy-two* words. The page includes the name of Allah seven times and Rabbi (Lord) twice. These serve as the days of the week and day and night, respectively.

Add 259, 43, and 72 to get 374. Subtract the 7 and 2 to get 365, the days of the solar year. The century mentioned in this verse may be measured in solar years. Could it be accidental? No.

259+43+72=374
374-(7+2) =365

*seventy-two has special meaning in the Quran, meaning three days.

Verse 281

وَاتَّقُوا يَوْمًا تُرْجَعُونَ فِيهِ إِلَى اللَّهِ ثُمَّ تُوَفَّىٰ كُلُّ نَفْسٍ مَّا كَسَبَتْ وَهُمْ لَا يُظْلَمُونَ (٢٨١)

And guard yourselves against a day in which ye will be brought back to Allah. Then every soul will be paid in full that which it hath earned, and they will not be wronged. (281)

This verse is the last verse of the Noble Quran and is on page 47. If 281 is grouped as 28 and 1, the sum is 29, which stands for the days of the lunar month, or February in a leap year. It is composed of 17 words. Adding 17 with 281, the sum is 298. Add 280 with 47 and 9, which is instances of the name of Allah and *Rabbi* (Lord) on the page, and the result is astonishing: 354, the days of the lunar year.

Could seventeen be the number of daily *rak'ah*s in Muslim prayers that we encountered in chapter one? It would make sense since prayers protect the Muslim.

28+1=29
281+17=298
298+47=345
345+9=354

Verse 60

وَإِذِ ٱسْتَسْقَىٰ مُوسَىٰ لِقَوْمِهِۦ فَقُلْنَا ٱضْرِب بِّعَصَاكَ ٱلْحَجَرَ ۖ فَٱنفَجَرَتْ مِنْهُ ٱثْنَتَا عَشْرَةَ عَيْنًا ۖ قَدْ عَلِمَ كُلُّ أُنَاسٍ مَّشْرَبَهُمْ ۖ كُلُوا۟ وَٱشْرَبُوا۟ مِن رِّزْقِ ٱللَّهِ وَلَا تَعْثَوْا۟ فِى ٱلْأَرْضِ مُفْسِدِينَ (٦٠)

And remember Moses prayed for water for his people; We said: «Strike the rock with thy staff.» Then gushed forth there from twelve springs. Each group knew its own place for water. So, eat and drink of the sustenance provided by Allah, and do no evil nor mischief on the (face of the) earth. (60)

Why does verse 60 refer to twelve springs? Why did Allah create the Sons of Israel in twelve sub-clans in the first place to burst from twelve springs?

The highlighted segment is composed of **sixty** letters. Wow! A strike is similar to a second, and sixty seconds form one minute, as sixty minutes create one hour. Are these time-related numbers coming spontaneously or are they planned intentionally? Realize Him.

The page number of this verse is nine, and it mentions Allah three times.

9+3=12.

Allah is made of four letters in the Arabic language, and if you multiply that with three, you get twelve.

4x3=12

It is amazing how Allah embedded these time-related numbers into the Quran.

The number 9(page) 6(6+0), and summed (9+6), is fifteen—half the days in a month. The amazing thing is, this verse contains time-related events and the number of years, and it has twenty-nine Arabic words in total. In the highlighted portion, it contains twenty-four words. Amazing!

Verse 233

وَٱلْوَٰلِدَٰتُ يُرْضِعْنَ أَوْلَٰدَهُنَّ حَوْلَيْنِ كَامِلَيْنِ ۖ لِمَنْ أَرَادَ أَن يُتِمَّ ٱلرَّضَاعَةَ ۚ وَعَلَى ٱلْمَوْلُودِ لَهُۥ رِزْقُهُنَّ وَكِسْوَتُهُنَّ بِٱلْمَعْرُوفِ ۚ لَا تُكَلَّفُ نَفْسٌ إِلَّا وُسْعَهَا ۚ لَا تُضَآرَّ وَٰلِدَةٌۢ بِوَلَدِهَا وَلَا مَوْلُودٌ لَّهُۥ بِوَلَدِهِۦ ۚ وَعَلَى ٱلْوَارِثِ مِثْلُ ذَٰلِكَ ۗ فَإِنْ أَرَادَا فِصَالًا عَن تَرَاضٍ مِّنْهُمَا وَتَشَاوُرٍ فَلَا جُنَاحَ عَلَيْهِمَا ۗ وَإِنْ أَرَدتُّمْ أَن تَسْتَرْضِعُوٓا۟ أَوْلَٰدَكُمْ فَلَا جُنَاحَ عَلَيْكُمْ إِذَا سَلَّمْتُم مَّآ ءَاتَيْتُم بِٱلْمَعْرُوفِ ۗ وَٱتَّقُوا۟ ٱللَّهَ وَٱعْلَمُوٓا۟ أَنَّ ٱللَّهَ بِمَا تَعْمَلُونَ بَصِيرٌ (٢٣٣)

Mothers shall suckle their children for two whole years; (that is) for those who wish to complete the suckling. The duty of feeding and clothing nursing mothers in a seemly manner is upon the father of the child. No-one should be charged beyond his capacity. A mother should not be made to suffer because of her child, nor should he to whom the child is born (be made to suffer) because of his child. And on the (father's) heir is incumbent the like of that (which was incumbent on the father). If they desire to wean the child by mutual consent and (after) consultation, it is no sin for them; and if ye wish to give your children out to nurse, it is no sin for you, provide

that ye pay what is due from you in kindness. Observe your duty to Allah, and know that Allah is Seer of what ye do. (233)

It is astonishing how this verse mathematically reflects what it describes. Allah orders breast feeding for two years, or twenty-four months in total. The explanation of the event in the highlighted part contains twenty-four Arabic words.

The verse number itself is breathtaking. Separate the verse number (233) into 2, 3, and 3. Multiply the sum of last two numbers (3+3) the result is 12. Multiplying by two, which is the rank of Al-Baqarah, and the product is twenty-four.

2x (3+3) =12
12x2=24

Yusuf (Joseph)

This surah is the twelfth in the Quran. It also lies between the twelfth and thirteenth chapter. What is amazing about this division?

If you look deeply into this surah's content, you will notice that Yusuf suffered humiliations from his brothers and his owners as a slave. After a long period of harassment, he won the love of the king and became the planning and financial minister of Egypt. The twelfth chapter describes his suffering, while the thirteenth chapter shows the beginning of his new life.

Let me go back to numbers related to time. Yusuf had eleven brothers(1+11=12) and the surah mentions him twenty-four times. The word 'dream' is repeated in surah Yusuf seven times. He, which refers to Allah, is also mentioned seven times. Lord

(*Rabbi* is the word in Arabic) is repeated thirteen times. This surah is in the twelfth and thirteenth chapters.

If you read and understand it correctly, you will see that this surah talks about every aspect of our lives through a full year (twelve months).

I don't want to list everything in Yusuf, only to present the different aspects of daily life. This is essential to show that their absence in a year would be alarming. The ecstasy of life is being happy and tolerating others, just as Yusuf was towards those who humiliated him personally, morally, and ethically.

Al- Room (Roma)

This surah is the thirtieth in the Quran and has sixty verses. One of the pages of surah Roma has the number of days in the solar year, 365. The sixty is directly correlated to seconds, minutes, and days in two months.

This surah is significant because it is the only one that contains all the words related to time mentioned in the Quran. For example, it mentions hours, day, night, morning, evening, year, sleep, the creation of living organisms, death, life, life after death, and more.

"In the day when the hour rises," or "in the day when the hour comes" are mentioned in many places in this surah. The hour is repeated many times in surah Roma. Is God saying that one hour is equal to sixty minutes and one minute is composed of sixty seconds? Why he is talking about hours in a surah that contains sixty verses and is ranked thirtieth in the Quran? Why does He connect hours with the number sixty?

This surah has the name of Allah twenty-nine times (including *Rabbi* and He). Is this coincidental? Why did God synchronize His words with time related-numbers?

If you look at page 405, the name of Allah is used six times. The word Allah in Arabic contains four letters. Multiplying 6 by 4 is 24. This page uses the word 'hour' two times, which in Arabic has six letters. 6 x 2 = 12.

The words 'day' and 'hour' are both contained in verses twelve and fourteen, and both are directly related to time.

Al-Mulk (The Kingdom)

This surah has thirty verses and Allah is repeated three times. If you multiply 3 by 4, you get 12. This represents the hours of a day or night, or the months in a year. The surah mentions beneficent or *Arrahman* (another name for Allah) four times. *Arrahman* in Arabic is spelled using six letters. If you multiply 6 by 4, you get 24. This represents the hours of a full day. These numbers are all related to time. Also, the surah cites Allah's pronoun, He, seven times.

3 x 4 = 12
6 x 4 = 24

Fussilat (Explained)

Surah Fussilat describes in a detailed way the creation of the world by Allah, which is done in six days. The word 'day' (*yawm*) is repeated six times. It could not be a coincidence. It is the work of the One who arranged the Quran.

Al-Qamar (The Moon)

(وَلَقَدْ يَسَّرْنَا ٱلْقُرْءَانَ لِلذِّكْرِ فَهَلْ مِن مُّدَّكِرٍ ٢٢)

And in truth We have made the Qur'an easy to remember; but is there any that remembereth? (22)

This surah is named after the moon. It is not accidental. Verses 17, 22, 31, and 40 repeat the same words. The amazing thing is that those repeated verses are each composed of thirty Arabic letters. Why? Because both the solar and the lunar months contain thirty days. Is this a coincidence? Allah named this surah "The Moon" and those verses contain thirty letters.

If you look deeply at those verse numbers and subtract them from each other, the differences are 5, 9, and 9. The sum of those numbers is 23. Add 1, which is the number of times Lord (*Rabbahu*) is mentioned, to get 24.

Although I am not looking at all chapters and *surahs* in the Quran, I am confident that it contains many math riddles and time-related puzzles waiting to be deciphered.

****

Analyzing the recurring numbers once more, we will notice an interesting correlation. Pages 12, 24, 29, 30, 31, 354, and 365 all include or mention time itself. It's amazing that the numbers that represent and govern our lives are shown to be important even in the Quran.

Furthermore, on page 365, the Quran states, "سِرَاجًا وَقَمَرًا مُّنِيرًا," which means, *"Hath placed therein a great lamp and a moon giving light!"* The Quran mentions the sun and moon on the page numbered for the days in a solar year. These numbers correlate to time, one way or another.

CHAPTER 3
CALENDARS IN THE QURAN

Mathematics is the science which uses easy words for hard ideas.

— *Edward Kasner and James R. Newman*

Let's look at the lunar and solar calendars. There are 365.242 days in the solar year, to be exact, and 354.367 days in the lunar year. The image below shows that if you multiply the numbers, then add the sums, and finally add both sums, you get the number of times Allah is mentioned in *Al-Tawba*, which is 169. What is the secret behind this? Is it simply a coincidence or the product of a mathematical genius?

In the fourth row of the top and lower bars is the number twelve. I will go deeply into these numbers. Why is this product the same as the number of times Allah is mentioned in this surah?

I named this style of calculating *farfalla*, which is the Italian word for butterfly. I used it on many occasions in my research, and often found perfect calculations that matched the notorious time-related numbers. I have selected two for demonstration purpose.

The *farfalla* style is a new system that I created specially on this purpose. It is close to a matrix in math but directed in a different way. On the other hand, if you review the classical calculator and using the *farfalla* style, you will notice that the sum of most numbers will be 15.

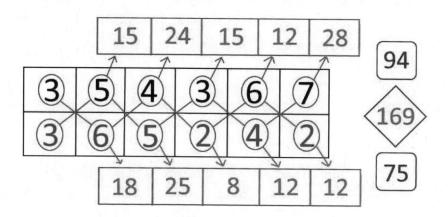

The top numbers are all related to time. Let's look at the repeated numbers of five or less in the lunar and solar years.

354.367 and 365.242

3, 3, 3, 4, 4, 5, 5

Seven numbers signify the days in a week. If you multiply the first and third numbers in the sequence, you get nine. If you multiply the fifth and seventh numbers in the sequence, you get twenty. If you add those, you get twenty-nine, which represents the number of days in a month. If you add up the least two numbers, 3 + 3, you get 6. If you multiply the highest two numbers together, 5+5, you get 25. If you add 6 with 25, you get 31.

3 + 3 = 6
5 x 5 = 25
6+25 = 31

This represents the number of days in a month. Now you can multiply the first and last, then add that with the product of the minimum and maximum. You get the number thirty, which also represents the number of days in a month.

3 x 5 = 15
3 x 5 = 15
15 + 15 = 30

If you multiply the largest two numbers and add that with the least number, you get twenty-eight, which represents the number of days in a month during a leap year. We have accounted for the number of days in all the months in a lunar and solar year through these numerical correlations.

5 x 5 = 25
25 + 3 = 28

If you multiply all the recurring numbers less than 5 and divide the maximum number found in all calculations, which is 31, and add 6, you get 354.387.

3 x 3 x 3 x 4 x 4 x 5 x 5 = 10,800
(10,800 / 31) + 6 = 354.387

This number is almost exactly the same as the days in a lunar year, with a small error margin of 0.02.

The words ٱلْيَوْمِ, يَوْمَ, and بِٱلْيَوْمِ are in surah *Al-Tawba* twelve times (*yawm* is 'day' in Arabic). This, of course, represents the number of months in a year. ٱلْيَوْمِ is mentioned in the surah six times and consists of five letters. 6 x 5 = 30, which represents number of days in a month. Take the word بِٱلْيَوْمِ and add the extra b or *ba* (Arabic alphabet) you will get thirty-one letters, which represents the days in a month.

يَوْمَ is mentioned in the surah six times. If you multiply the number of times it's mentioned and the number of letters in the word, you get eighteen. Then, if you add the result of the previous calculation, you get forty-eight. Then divide the number by two to get twenty-four, which represents the hours in a day. The number is divided by two because of its double meaning.

The word عام (year) is mentioned four times and contains three letters. 4 X 3 = 12, which means the number of months in a year.

Allah, as we said before, is mentioned 169 times in surah *Al-Tawba*, but there are other words used to refer to Him. For example, رب (Lord), هُوَ (He), and إِلَـٰهٌ (God) are mentioned seven times each.

Verse 36 of surah *Al-Tawba* mentions Allah three times. If you divide the number of the verse by the number of times the verse mentions Allah (36/3), you get twelve, which is the number of months in a year. In the coming chapters, I will demonstrate how miraculous it is that each surah is directly related to correct numbers in time.

CHAPTER 4
THE QURAN NUMBERS CONFORMITY WITH THE TIME

If two wrongs don't make a right, try three.

~ Unknown

Most verses in the Quran that mention the sun, moon, day, and night coincide to numbers of the week, months (both lunar and solar), or half months (days or weeks). The astounding thing about the Quran is that time-related numbers like 7, 12, 14, 15, 24, 28, 29, 30, 31, 177, 354, and 365 correlate to the number of verses or the rank or number of surahs, the number of verses on a page, and so on.

In this chapter, we'll review a series of verses in which God describes time-related numbers.

Al-Israa (The Night Journey)

وَجَعَلْنَا ٱلَّيْلَ وَٱلنَّهَارَ ءَايَتَيْنِۖ فَمَحَوْنَآ ءَايَةَ ٱلَّيْلِ وَجَعَلْنَآ ءَايَةَ ٱلنَّهَارِ مُبْصِرَةً لِّتَبْتَغُواْ فَضْلًا مِّن رَّبِّكُمْ وَلِتَعْلَمُواْ عَدَدَ ٱلسِّنِينَ وَٱلْحِسَابَۚ

(وَكُلَّ شَىْءٍ فَصَّلْنَـٰهُ تَفْصِيلًا ١٢)

And We appoint the night and the day two portents. Then We make dark the portent of the night, and We make the portent

of the day sight-giving, that ye may seek bounty from your Lord, and that ye may know the computation of the years, and the reckoning; and everything has We expounded with a clear expounding. (12)

There are twenty-nine Arabic words in this verse, which represents the number of days in the lunar month. If you count the highlighted words, you get twenty-four. This represents the hours in a full day. Don't forget the number of verse 12; this represents the hours in a night or day, or months of the year. What is the wisdom behind this? Who can construct these sophistication patterns?

Allah emphasizes in the Quran that mathematics originated from calculations relating to years, months, minutes, and seconds.

Yunas (Jonah)

هُوَ ٱلَّذِى جَعَلَ ٱلشَّمْسَ ضِيَآءً وَٱلْقَمَرَ نُورًا وَقَدَّرَهُ مَنَازِلَ لِتَعْلَمُوا۟ عَدَدَ ٱلسِّنِينَ وَٱلْحِسَابَ ۚ مَا خَلَقَ ٱللَّهُ ذَٰلِكَ إِلَّا بِٱلْحَقِّ ۚ يُفَصِّلُ ٱلْءَايَٰتِ لِقَوْمٍ يَعْلَمُونَ (٥) إِنَّ فِى ٱخْتِلَٰفِ ٱلَّيْلِ وَٱلنَّهَارِ وَمَا خَلَقَ ٱللَّهُ فِى ٱلسَّمَٰوَٰتِ وَٱلْأَرْضِ لَءَايَٰتٍ لِّقَوْمٍ يَتَّقُونَ (٦)

He it is Who appointed the sun a splendor and the moon a light, and measured for her stages, that ye might know the number of the years, and the reckoning. Allah created not (all) that save in truth. He detailed the revelations for people who have knowledge. (5) Lo! in the difference of day and night and all that Allah hath created in the heavens and the earth are portents, verily, for folk who ward off (evil). (6)

Surat Jonah *(Yunus)* mentions Allah sixty-one times and *Rabbi* twenty-four times, which is phenomenal. This represents the twenty-four hours in a full day. The highlighted verse contains sixty-one letters exactly. Why do these numbers show up in places that we would otherwise consider unimportant? If we divide 365, the number of days in the solar year, by 61, we get 11.967, which is approximately 12.

Next, take away the number of times that it mentions Allah on every page. You will get 29.

5,2,6,3,5,5,4,8,8,3,5,1,4,2 ⇨ 1,2,3,4,5,6,8
1 + 2 + 3 + 4 + 5 + 6 + 8 = 29

If we multiply all the numbers together instead of adding, we get 5760. If you divide that by 24, we get 240. Then if we subtract 240 from 354 (the days in the lunar year), we get 114—the number of surahs in the Quran.

$1 \times 2 \times 3 \times 4 \times 5 \times 6 \times 8 = 5760$

$\frac{5760}{24} = 240$

$354 - 240 = 114$

An-Nahl (The Bees)

وَسَخَّرَ لَكُمُ ٱلَّيْلَ وَٱلنَّهَارَ وَٱلشَّمْسَ وَٱلْقَمَرَ وَٱلنُّجُومُ مُسَخَّرَاتٌ بِأَمْرِهِ ۗ إِنَّ فِى ذَٰلِكَ لَءَايَٰتٍ لِّقَوْمٍ يَعْقِلُونَ (١٢)

And He hath constrained the night and the day and the sun and the moon to be of service unto you, and the stars are made subservient by His command. Lo! Herein indeed are portents for people who have sense. (12)

The portion highlighted consists of thirty letters, which represents the days in a month. Also, the verse is the twelfth in the surah *An-Nahl,* which represents the hours in a day or night. This is significant because Allah mentions day and night in this verse.

Al-Ma'ida (The Table)

وَلَقَدْ أَخَذَ ٱللَّهُ مِيثَٰقَ بَنِىٓ إِسْرَٰٓءِيلَ وَبَعَثْنَا مِنْهُمُ ٱثْنَىْ عَشَرَ نَقِيبًا ۖ وَقَالَ ٱللَّهُ إِنِّى مَعَكُمْ ۖ لَئِنْ أَقَمْتُمُ ٱلصَّلَوٰةَ وَءَاتَيْتُمُ ٱلزَّكَوٰةَ وَءَامَنتُم بِرُسُلِى وَعَزَّرْتُمُوهُمْ وَأَقْرَضْتُمُ ٱللَّهَ قَرْضًا حَسَنًا لَّأُكَفِّرَنَّ عَنكُمْ سَيِّـَٔاتِكُمْ وَلَأُدْخِلَنَّكُمْ جَنَّٰتٍ تَجْرِى مِن تَحْتِهَا ٱلْأَنْهَٰرُ ۚ فَمَن كَفَرَ بَعْدَ ذَٰلِكَ مِنكُمْ فَقَدْ ضَلَّ سَوَآءَ ٱلسَّبِيلِ (١٢)

Allah made a covenant of old with the Children of Israel and We raised among them twelve Chieftains, and Allah said: Lo! I am with you. If ye establish worship and pay the poor-due, and believe in My messengers and support them, and lend unto Allah a kindly loan, surely, I shall remit your sins, and surely, I shall bring you into gardens underneath which rivers flow. Whoso among you disbelieved after this will go astray from a plain road. (12)

Numerous stories show the events that happened to the Jews people. They were twelve sub-tribes. When Allah saved them from Pharaoh's humiliations, Allah served them food and water. The source of water was twelve in number. As well as twelve chiefs that Allah chosen as Moses supporters.

Why does Allah talk about twelve chieftains in verse 12? Is it coincidence, or did He choose this intentionally?

Al-Noor (The Light)

Surah Al-Noor is the twenty-fourth in the Quran. This represents the total hours of one full day. This surah contains a page numbered 354, the days of the lunar year.

It cannot be coincidental that one of the pages in this surah has the most abundant use of the word light (*Noor*), which is named after this surah. It is repeated five times in one verse, which is 35th. Dividing 35 with 5 is 7. Not enough? The most amazing thing is that the word light in this surah is repeated seven times—the days of the week.

Allah is mentioned in this surah eighty times, He (*Huwa*) is used once. Page 354 (the lunar year) mentions Allah ten times. Added together, the sum is 355. Add the remainder, the uses of He (*Huwa*), to get 365 for the total days of the solar year.

Furthermore, by adding numbers like the rank of the surah, the total verses, and the number of times Allah is mentioned, we get 169. That was the same number of times Allah was mentioned in surah *Al-Tawba*, my favorite surah, which describes the basic concepts of time.

354
354+11=365
24+64+81=169

Daha

فَٱصْبِرْ عَلَىٰ مَا يَقُولُونَ وَسَبِّحْ بِحَمْدِ رَبِّكَ قَبْلَ طُلُوعِ ٱلشَّمْسِ وَقَبْلَ غُرُوبِهَا
(وَمِنْ ءَانَآئِ ٱلَّيْلِ فَسَبِّحْ وَأَطْرَافَ ٱلنَّهَارِ لَعَلَّكَ تَرْضَىٰ) ١٣٠

Therefore, be patient with what they say and celebrate (constantly) the praises of thy Lord before the rising of the sun, and before its setting; yea, celebrate them for part of the hours of the night, and at the sides of the day: that thou mayest have (spiritual) joy. (130)

This verse is composed of twenty-four Arabic words. It talks about the sun rising and setting, and the hours of the day and night. Having the number twenty-four occur here is marvelous. Who could be behind this correlation?

Al-Araf (The Heights)

This surah is seventh in the Quran and is composed of 206 verses. We understand by now that seven represents the days of the week, but what's impressive is how this surah conforms to other time-related numbers. Allah put this surah in the seventh place to show that He did not choose these numbers randomly, but consciously aligned them to conform to time-related numbers.

Let's use some tricky math. By omitting the zero in the number of verses and multiplying 2 x 6, the product is 12—one of the time-related numbers. There are seven prophets mentioned in its pages: Adam, Noah, Hud, Salah, Lot, Shuaib, and Moses. It also mentions Muhammad indirectly, but not by name. Dividing 206 by 7 is just over 29.

It mentions Allah, Lord, and He 61, 64, and 7 times, respectively. Multiplied together, the product is 27328. The root of 27328 is 165. Doubling 165 is 330. Adding 330 with 24* is 354, the days of the lunar year. When cubed, 27328 is just over 30, the days in one month. If separated individually and added together, the sum of the individual numbers in 27328 is 29, the days of the lunar month. Multiplied, their product is 672. By dividing 672 by 2, we get 336. Add 336 and 29 to get 365, the days of the solar year.

*Verse 24 describes the first day humans landed on the earth.

(2+0) x6=12
61x64x7=27328
√27328=165
165x2=330
330+24=354
³√27328≈30
2+7+3+2+8=29
2x7x3x2x8=672
672/2=336
336+29=365

Al-Araf

قَالَ ٱهْبِطُواْ بَعْضُكُمْ لِبَعْضٍ عَدُوٌّ وَلَكُمْ فِى ٱلْأَرْضِ مُسْتَقَرٌّ وَمَتَـٰعٌ إِلَىٰ حِينٍ (٢٤)

He said: Go down (from hence), one of you a foe unto the other. There will be for you on earth a habitation and provision for a while. (24)

Verse 24, the number of which represents the hours in a day and night, contains fourteen words. Fourteen is half the letters in the Arabic language.

A strange question: how many times do humans live?

The answer from religious people is clear. God indirectly suggests that humans have one full life, with half on earth and the other half in the afterlife. Fourteen is also half the days in each month. The question remains, why did God choose the number fourteen to describe the introduction of human settlement on earth, as well as their transition into the afterlife?

Although the creation of humans in the Bible, Torah, and Quran are contradictory to the theory of evolution, Allah explained how He created Adam and Eva and how they came to earth to inhabit. After they disobeyed His orders in the paradise, they were kicked out from the Garden with Lucifer.

Since that point, human death is inevitable. After passing away, what is next? Another life. In this case, Allah explains the start of human life on earth with verse 24!

Verse 144

قَالَ يَٰمُوسَىٰٓ إِنِّى ٱصْطَفَيْتُكَ عَلَى ٱلنَّاسِ بِرِسَٰلَٰتِى وَبِكَلَٰمِى فَخُذْ مَآ ءَاتَيْتُكَ وَكُن مِّنَ ٱلشَّٰكِرِينَ (١٤٤)

He said: O Moses! I have preferred thee above mankind by My messages and by My speaking (unto thee). So, hold that which I have given thee, and be among the thankful. (144)

God chooses Moses (AS) by speaking directly to him and granting him the book (*Torah*) in a verse relevant to time. This couldn't have been a coincidence. The square root of 144 is 12! If you take the page number of this verse and combine it with common time-related numbers, you will see the wisdom behind the Quran's relationship with time. The page number is 168 and the verse number is 144. Subtracting 144 from 168 is 24.

In this surah, the name of Moses is repeated twenty-one times. $21 = 3 \times 7$.

Why did Allah code these verses, or the Quran in general, in a complex way that mathematically reveals time-related numbers? Is there a secret behind the Arabic language and its mathematical correlations with time?

$\sqrt{144}=12$
168-144=24
21= 7+7+7

Verse 180

(وَلِلَّهِ ٱلْأَسْمَاءُ ٱلْحُسْنَىٰ فَٱدْعُوهُ بِهَا ۖ وَذَرُوا۟ ٱلَّذِينَ يُلْحِدُونَ فِىٓ أَسْمَـٰٓئِهِۦ ۚ سَيُجْزَوْنَ مَا كَانُوا۟ يَعْمَلُونَ ١٨٠)

Allah›s are the fairest names. Invoke Him by them. And leave the company of those who blaspheme His names. They will be requited what they do. (180)

This verse describes the best names of Allah. The page number of this verse is 174. Adding the verse number, 180, with the page number gives 354, the days of lunar year.

180+174=354

This surah mentions eight animals. If you leave out the calf, which is the only animal that was made of gold, you get seven animals. This represents the days in a week. This surah also mentions Saturday, the seventh day of the Jewish week.

Al-Kahf (The Cave)

(وَلَبِثُوا۟ فِى كَهْفِهِمْ ثَلَـٰثَ مِا۟ئَةٍ سِنِينَ وَٱزْدَادُوا۟ تِسْعًا ٢٥)

And (it is said) they tarried in their cave three hundred years and add nine. (25)

Allah states that they stayed in the cave for 309 years. If you repeat the numbers, excluding the zero, you get 3, 3, 9, 9. Multiply all of them together to get 729, then divide by 2 because if we doubled the numbers (309) then we must divide by 2. This gives us the number of days in the solar year.

309 years

3 x 3 x 9 x 9 = 729
729/2 = 364.5~365

Verse 22

سَيَقُولُونَ ثَلَاثَةٌ رَّابِعُهُمْ كَلْبُهُمْ وَيَقُولُونَ خَمْسَةٌ سَادِسُهُمْ كَلْبُهُمْ رَجْمًا بِالْغَيْبِ وَيَقُولُونَ سَبْعَةٌ وَثَامِنُهُمْ كَلْبُهُمْ قُل رَّبِّي أَعْلَمُ بِعِدَّتِهِم مَّا يَعْلَمُهُمْ إِلَّا قَلِيلٌ فَلَا تُمَارِ فِيهِمْ إِلَّا مِرَاءً ظَاهِرًا وَلَا تَسْتَفْتِ فِيهِم مِّنْهُمْ أَحَدًا (٢٢)

(Some) will say: They were three, their dog the fourth, and (some) say: Five, their dog the sixth, guessing at random; and (some) say: Seven, and their dog the eighth. Say (O Muhammad): My Lord is best aware of their number. None knoweth them save a few. So, contend not concerning them except with an outward contending, and ask not any of them to pronounce concerning them. (22)

I gathered the numbers discussed in verse 22 and made some calculations using my *farfalla* method. I separated the numbers based on each statement: 3 with 4, 5 with 6, and 7 with 8.

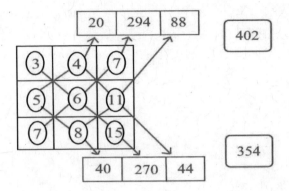

If you add each pair together, you get, 7, 11, and 15. Then by using the *farfalla* method, I multiplied them to get numbers related to seconds, minutes, a full day (24), day or night (12), and the days in a lunar year (354).

If you add the least two sums, you get sixty. This represents the minutes in an hour or the seconds in a minute.

20 + 40 = 60

If you subtract the greatest two sums (294 and 270), you get twenty-four, the hours in a full day.

294 - 270 = 24

Subtract the sum of the sums to get forty-eight, then divide the new sum by two (since you're working with two numbers):

(402 - 354)/ 2 = 24

Although the verse is not related to time, I was curious and looked up if such numbers in the Quran randomly coincide with time. They fit with my expectations.

Al-An'am (The Cattle)

فَالِقُ ٱلْإِصْبَاحِ وَجَعَلَ ٱلَّيْلَ سَكَنًا وَٱلشَّمْسَ وَٱلْقَمَرَ حُسْبَانًا ۚ ذَٰلِكَ تَقْدِيرُ ٱلْعَزِيزِ ٱلْعَلِيمِ (٩٦)

He it is that cleaveth the daybreak (from the dark): He makes the night for rest and tranquility, and the sun and moon for the reckoning (of time): such is the judgment and ordering of (Him), the Exalted in Power, the Omniscient. (96)

This verse contains fifteen Arabic words, or half the days of the month. Add the number of this verse with the number of the page it's on, 140+96, to get 236. If you subtract 354 from 236, the result is 118, which is a third of the lunar year. Multiply 118 by 3 to get 354.

Verse 96 has fifteen words and talks about the night, which is half of a day. It contains sixty letters, which represents the seconds in a minute or minutes in an hour.

The number 96 itself has a total of fifteen (9+6) = 15. What genius is this?

Verse 13

(وَلَهُ مَا سَكَنَ فِى ٱلَّيْلِ وَٱلنَّهَارِ ۚ وَهُوَ ٱلسَّمِيعُ ٱلْعَلِيمُ) (١٣)

Unto Him belongeth whatsoever resteth in the night and the day. He is the Hearer, the Knower. (13)

This verse briefly mentions a topic related to time. It contains twelve words and thirty-six letters. 36 − 12 = 24. How can we understand the mathematical logic behind verses that explain day and night, the sun and moon, or death and life? Why they are coded like this?

This verse is on page 129. If these numbers are added together, the sum is 12. The pronoun of Allah, هو He (*Huwa*), is used six times on this page. This word is composed in two letters. Multiplied together, the product is 12. The letters of Allah and Lord total 14.

Luqman

Surah *Luqman* is thirty-first in the Quran and contains twenty-nine words. It discusses how Allah extends or shortens the day and night and how He subdued the sun and moon. The concept of time came from celestial movements and these numbers represent the days in the solar and lunar months. They are related to time, and the number of verses is not a coincidence. It is the work of the One, of Allah. He knows what He is talking about. His words are distinct from those of humans.

Verse 34

إِنَّ ٱللَّهَ عِندَهُۥ عِلْمُ ٱلسَّاعَةِ وَيُنَزِّلُ ٱلْغَيْثَ وَيَعْلَمُ مَا فِى ٱلْأَرْحَامِ ۖ وَمَا تَدْرِى نَفْسٌ مَّاذَا تَكْسِبُ غَدًا ۖ وَمَا تَدْرِى نَفْسٌ بِأَىِّ أَرْضٍ تَمُوتُ ۚ إِنَّ ٱللَّهَ عَلِيمٌ خَبِيرٌ (٣٤)

Lo! Allah! With Him is knowledge of the Hour. He sendeth down the rain, and knoweth that which is in the wombs. No soul knoweth what it will earn to-morrow, and no soul knoweth in what land it will die. Lo! Allah is Knower, Aware. (34)

There are thirty-one words in this verse, which represents the number of days in a month. This verse is about fundamental faith in the Islamic religion. If you multiply three by four (in the verse number), you get twelve, which represents the number of hours in a day or night.

Verse 24

(نُمَتِّعُهُمْ قَلِيلًا ثُمَّ نَضْطَرُّهُمْ إِلَىٰ عَذَابٍ غَلِيظٍ ٢٤)

We give them comfort for a little, and then We drive them to a heavy doom. (24)

Look at the number of this verse and count its letters. It states that the leisure sinners find on earth will eventually lead to their doom. Why is it in this verse? We have seven words, thirty letters, and twenty-four, the number of this verse!

Life itself is a leisure. Leisure is not eternal, it ends someday if not invested in a correct way it leads to a hellfire in the day of judgement.

Verse 29

(أَلَمْ تَرَ أَنَّ ٱللَّهَ يُولِجُ ٱلَّيْلَ فِى ٱلنَّهَارِ وَيُولِجُ ٱلنَّهَارَ فِى ٱلَّيْلِ وَسَخَّرَ ٱلشَّمْسَ وَٱلْقَمَرَ كُلٌّ يَجْرِى إِلَىٰٓ أَجَلٍ مُّسَمًّى وَأَنَّ ٱللَّهَ بِمَا تَعْمَلُونَ خَبِيرٌ ٢٩)

Hast thou not seen how Allah causeth the night to pass into the day and causeth the day to pass into the night, and hath subdued the sun and the moon (to do their work), each running unto an appointed term; and that Allah is aware of what ye do? (29)

The interchange of the day and the night and Allah's power over the sun and moon in the twenty-ninth verse is amazing. The miracle doesn't stop there. Count the Arabic words; there are exactly twenty-nine. How could this be coincidental? It is phenomenal!

Al-Imran (The Family of Imran)

إِنَّ فِى خَلْقِ ٱلسَّمَـٰوَٰتِ وَٱلْأَرْضِ وَٱخْتِلَـٰفِ ٱلَّيْلِ وَٱلنَّهَارِ لَـَٔايَـٰتٍ لِّأُو۟لِى ٱلْأَلْبَـٰبِ (١٩٠)

Behold! In the creation of the heavens and the earth, and the alternation of Night and Day — there are indeed Signs for men of understanding. (190)

The day and night are each half of twenty-four hours. This verse has fourteen words, which is half of the days in a month. The verse itself is composed of fourteen Arabic words.

The root of 190, the number of the verse, is close to 14.

$\sqrt{190} = 13.78 \approx 14$

Surat Ana'am

قُل لِّمَن مَّا فِى ٱلسَّمَـٰوَٰتِ وَٱلْأَرْضِ ۖ قُل لِّلَّهِ ۚ كَتَبَ عَلَىٰ نَفْسِهِ ٱلرَّحْمَةَ ۚ لَيَجْمَعَنَّكُمْ إِلَىٰ يَوْمِ ٱلْقِيَـٰمَةِ لَا رَيْبَ فِيهِ ۚ ٱلَّذِينَ خَسِرُوٓا۟ أَنفُسَهُمْ فَهُمْ لَا يُؤْمِنُونَ (١٢)

Say: Unto whom belongeth whatsoever is in the heavens and the earth? Say: Unto Allah. He hath prescribed for Himself mercy, that He may bring you all together to the Day of Resurrection whereof there is no doubt. Those who ruin their souls will not believe. (12)

I wonder why most verses that contain day or night or the sun or the moon contain time-related numbers. This verse is a good example.

Verse 12 and word "day" are in the same area!

RECITAL PROSTRATIONS *(SUJOOD ATTILAWA)*

This reading holds special meaning among Muslims. It is astonishing how the prostrations mentioned in the Quran, outside the daily prayers, are arranged. Their places in the Quran, the verses they contain, their meaning, and number of times Allah is mentioned all relate to the concept of time.

Table 3

Name of the Surat	Verse #	# of Allah, letters, and others / page
Araf	206	7 Allah, 48 letters
Al-rad	15	9 Allah
Al-Nahl	49	12 Allah
Al-Isra	109	7 Allah, 30 letters
Maryam	58	6 Allah
Hajj	18	7 Allah, 1 rabbi, sun and moon
Hajj	77	12 Allah and related
Al-Furqan	60	7 Rabbi and Rahman
Al-Naml	25	7 Allah
As-Sajda	15	7 Allah, 30 verses
Saad	24	--
Fussilat	37	7 Allah, night and day, sun and moon
Al-Najm	62	15 letters, sun and moon
Al-Inshiqaq	21	7 words
Al-Alaq	19	--

The numerical and time correlations in the Quran

If you look at the above table listing the verses that demand prostration (*sujood*), you will notice they are both talking about time, or their numbers and words/letters that are related to time.

The total prostrations (*sujoods*) in the Quran is fifteen, half of the days of the month. Has this happened by chance?

You can find our usual numbers like 7, 12, 15, 24, 30, 48, and 60 here too. Again, notice that many verses in the table describe time, the sun, moon, day, and night.

First, the Quran has two types of verses: *Makki* and *Madani*. When the Quran first came to Mecca, it focused on a handful of things like the afterlife, judgement day, conflict with polytheism, previous messengers, morals, and most importantly, the idea that Allah is not accompanied by other gods. This is a completely different structure when compared to the Quran after it came to Medina. It began to focus more on law, business, family, hypocrisy, and conflict with other religions. In Surah Haj, there are two prostrations (*sujoods*). This could reflect the Quran and how there are two types of conceptual structures, *Makki* and *Madani*.

Surah *Haj* combines these two types. I would like to draw your attention in the highlighted text, surah *Al-Furqan*, which stands exactly in the middle of the rank. It means 'differentiator' in Arabic.

In this observation, it's exciting to see the Quran's precise conformity with time. As I mentioned before, I can't figure this relationship out; however, I do believe that there is a superior intelligence responsible for these correlations.

CHAPTER 5
THE RELATIONSHIP BETWEEN TIME AND THE QURAN'S CONSERVATION

Go down deep enough into anything and you will find mathematics.

~Dean Schlicter

Looking deeply at the verses that articulate the conservation of the Quran and its eminence, you will notice they connect regularly to time-related numbers.

The majority of the Quran's readers pass through it superficially, so I would like to recommend going deeply into the wisdom behind these numbers and how they related to each other. Read. Feel. Interpret. Evaluate. Calculate. Believe.

If you look deeply into the Quran, you will notice that choosing Arabic was not a random act. There is a phenomenal perfection in this language.

Let's look at some verses.

Al Hijr (The Stoneland)

(إِنَّا نَحْنُ نَزَّلْنَا ٱلذِّكْرَ وَإِنَّا لَهُ لَحَٰفِظُونَ ٩)

Lo! We, even We, reveal the Reminder, and lo! We verily are its Guardian. (9)

This verse contains twenty-nine letters in seven *alifs* and seven *noons*. Surah *Hijr* contains ninety-nine verses. There are nine mentions of the word Lord (*rabbi*) and two mentions of the word Allah in this surah. The sum of these words is eleven. In the entire surah, *Rabbak* is mentioned six times and it contains three letters. Rabbi contains two letters and is mentioned twice in the surah. Finally, his Lord (*Rabihi*) is mentioned once and contains three letters.

If you multiply the ninety-nine verses by the seven *alifs* and divide the sum by two, then add seven for the *noons*, the result will be days of the lunar year.

$((99 \times 7)/2) + 7 = 353.5$

If we round the number, we get the lunar year, which is 354 days.

If you add the mentions of rabbi and Allah from the surah (eleven):

$353.5 + 11 = 364.5$

Once rounded, the number represents the solar year. Multiply 7 by 2 to get 14, and 7 by 9 to get 63. If you multiply 14 by 63, the result is 882.

The Relationship Between Time And The Quran's Conservation

7 x 9 = 63
7 x 2 = 14
14 x 63 = 882
√882 = 29.7 ~ 30

The square root of that number is 29.7, which rounds up to 30. If you subtract 14 from 63, you get 49, and its square root is 7. By adding 63 to 14, you get 77, but if you divide that by the number of times Rabbi and Allah are mentioned in the surah, you get 7.

63 + 14 = 77
77/11 = 7

If you multiply 7 and 7 and add 11, you get 60.

(7 x 7) +11 = 60

Throughout all these calculations, we have seen a theme for the results. All these numbers refer to time, for example 60 seconds, 60 minutes, 1 hour, 12 hours, 24 hours, 1 month (28– 31 days), and 12 months (1 year). Where do these correlations come from?

If we multiply the number of times the verse mentions *Rabbak, Rabbi,* and *Rabbihi,* which is 6, 2, 1, you get 12. This represents twelve months in a year or twelve hours in a day.

6 x 2 x 1 = 12

Although, this is not directly related to time, it talks about the preservation of the Quran, which means that as times goes on, it will remain consistent in its meaning and authenticity.

Verse 87

(وَلَقَدْ ءَاتَيْنَٰكَ سَبْعًا مِّنَ ٱلْمَثَانِى وَٱلْقُرْءَانَ ٱلْعَظِيمَ ۸۷)

We have given thee seven of the oft-repeated (verses) and the great Qur›an. (87)

If you look at the highlighted part in this verse, you will count twenty-four letters, with fourteen remaining. Fourteen represents two weeks and twenty-four represents the hours in a full day. The seven pairs are fourteen. Strange combinations. 24/7!

Verse 1

(الٓرٰ تِلْكَ ءَايَٰتُ ٱلْكِتَٰبِ وَقُرْءَانٍ مُّبِينٍ ۱)

Alif. Lam. Ra. These are verses of the Scripture(Text) and a plain Reading. (1)

This verse consists of seven words. It preaches about the Quran and its marvels. The Quran is clear despite skepticism from some about its divine origin. For example, Thomas Carlyle called the Quran «toilsome reading and a wearisome confused jumble, crude, incondite» with «endless iterations, long-windedness, entanglement» and «insupportable stupidity.»[4] The mathematically balanced words in this short verse and the Quran as a whole remain the most monumental testimony that the Quran is the authentic word of God. The question is; how does the Quran looks like?

The Biggest Five Challenges

---

4   Thomas Carlyle (1841), *On Heroes, Hero-Worship and the Heroic in History*, p. 64-67

The Relationship Between Time And The Quran's Conservation

Many verses challenge the skeptics, who claim that Muhammad wrote the Quran or that it was borrowed from other religions. Yes, the Torah and the Bible are revelations from Allah, as well as the Quran.

After all these centuries, we have never heard anyone who claimed to fabricate the Quran or something like it. Why? There is nothing even close.

Let's look at how the Quran challenges these allegations.

1) **Al-Isra** (The Night Journey)

قُل لَّئِنِ ٱجْتَمَعَتِ ٱلْإِنسُ وَٱلْجِنُّ عَلَىٰٓ أَن يَأْتُوا۟ بِمِثْلِ هَـٰذَا ٱلْقُرْءَانِ لَا يَأْتُونَ بِمِثْلِهِۦ وَلَوْ كَانَ بَعْضُهُمْ لِبَعْضٍ ظَهِيرًا (٨٨)

Say: «If the whole of mankind and Jinn were to gather together to produce the like of this Qurʾan, they could not produce the like thereof, even if they backed up each other with help and support. (88)

Look at this verse seriously. It is the eighty-eighth verse in the surah. In addition, it is also the seventeenth in the Quran. If you add those numbers together—1, 7, 8, and 8—you get twenty-four, which represents the hours in a full day.

1+7+8+8=24
Or
1x7=7
8x3=24

2) **Al-Baqarah**

وَإِن كُنتُمْ فِى رَيْبٍ مِّمَّا نَزَّلْنَا عَلَىٰ عَبْدِنَا فَأْتُوا۟ بِسُورَةٍ مِّن مِّثْلِهِۦ وَٱدْعُوا۟ شُهَدَآءَكُم مِّن دُونِ ٱللَّهِ إِن كُنتُمْ صَـٰدِقِينَ (٢٣)

And if ye are in doubt as to what We have revealed from time to time to Our servant, then produce a Surah like thereunto; and call your witnesses or helpers (if there are any) besides Allah, if your (doubts) are true. (23)

This verse, numbered twenty-three, is second in the Quran-Al Baqarah. If you multiply all those numbers (2, 2, 3), you get twelve.

3) Hud

أَمْ يَقُولُونَ ٱفْتَرَىٰهُ قُلْ فَأْتُواْ بِعَشْرِ سُوَرٍ مِّثْلِهِ مُفْتَرَيَاتٍ وَٱدْعُواْ مَنِ ٱسْتَطَعْتُم مِّن دُونِ ٱللَّهِ إِن كُنتُمْ صَادِقِينَ (١٣)

Or they may say «He forged it.» Say «Bring ye then ten Suras forged, like unto it, and call (to your aid) whomsoever ye can, other than Allah! — if ye speak the truth! (13)

Surah Hud is at the eleventh position in the Quran. Add both numbers (13+11) to get twenty-four.

13 is the number of verse and 11 is the rank of surah Hud.

13+11=24

4) Yunas

وَمَا كَانَ هَٰذَا ٱلْقُرْءَانُ أَن يُفْتَرَىٰ مِن دُونِ ٱللَّهِ وَلَٰكِن تَصْدِيقَ ٱلَّذِى بَيْنَ يَدَيْهِ وَتَفْصِيلَ ٱلْكِتَابِ لاَ رَيْبَ فِيهِ مِن رَّبِّ ٱلْعَالَمِينَ (٣٧) أَمْ يَقُولُونَ ٱفْتَرَىٰهُ قُلْ فَأْتُواْ بِسُورَةٍ مِّثْلِهِ وَٱدْعُواْ مَنِ ٱسْتَطَعْتُم مِّن دُونِ ٱللَّهِ إِن كُنتُمْ صَادِقِينَ (٣٨)

And this Quran is not such as could ever be invented despite of Allah; but it is a confirmation of that which was before it and an exposition of that which is decreed for mankind - Therein is no doubt - from the Lord of the universes. (37) Or

say they: He hath invented it? Say: Then bring a surah like unto it, and call (for help) on all ye can besides Allah, if ye are truthful. (38)

Surah Jonah (*Yunus*) is the tenth in the Quran. There are two verses in this section. If we arrange these numbers as 10:37:38, it shows the rank of the surah and the two verses explaining the challenge from Allah to design something identical to the Quran. Multiplying these numbers, the product is 14060. The cube root of 14060 is 24.

$$10 \times 37 \times 38 = 14060$$
$$\sqrt[3]{14060} = 24$$

Amazing math!

5) **Al-Ankabut** (The spider)

وَمَا كُنتَ تَتْلُواْ مِن قَبْلِهِ مِن كِتَٰبٍ وَلَا تَخُطُّهُ بِيَمِينِكَ ۖ إِذًا لَّٱرْتَابَ ٱلْمُبْطِلُونَ (٤٨)

And thou wast not (able) to recite a Book before this (Book came) nor art thou (able) to transcribe it with thy right hand: in that case, indeed, would the talkers of vanities have doubted. (48)

This is the greatest objection to those claiming that the Prophet Mohamed wrote the Quran: he was illiterate. This will not silence the critics, who argue the Quran is not authentic and not a revelation from Allah. If the Prophet Mohammed could neither read nor write, how could he have orchestrated this noble book?

On the other hand, what is fascinating in this verse is not its challenge, but how it conforms mathematically with concepts of time.

Surat *Al-Ankabut* is twenty-ninth in the Quran, representing the days of the lunar month. The verse number is forty-eight, which is the number of hours in two days. Allah mentioned two features of Mohammed, one of which was that he couldn't read or write. Each skill can be represented as one day, for a total of two days!

Why are these verses always related to time? The page number of this verse is 402. If you subtract 48 from 402, you get 354, exactly the number of days in the lunar year. Take (12x12) +(12x12) to get 288. Subtract that from 402 and the result is 114, which is the number of surahs in the Quran. Forty-eight is composed of two numbers (4+8) that total twelve.

4+8=12
24+24=48
402-48=354
402-288=114

Al-Ana'am

(وَتَمَّتْ كَلِمَتُ رَبِّكَ صِدْقًا وَعَدْلًا لَّا مُبَدِّلَ لِكَلِمَاتِهِ ۚ وَهُوَ السَّمِيعُ الْعَلِيمُ) (١١٥)

The Word of thy Lord doth find its fulfilment in truth and in justice: none can change His Words: for He is the one who heareth and knoweth all. (115)

The highlighted portion of this text contains seven words, which represents the days of the week.

The Relationship Between Time And The Quran's Conservation

The expression of this verse is intense because His words are eternal and absolutely the truth. When analyzed using the concept of time, we get another miracle: 7 and 14 gives the total number of Arabic words in the verse.

Verse number 115 shows another wonder too. Separating these numbers and adding them together gives seven.

1+1+5=7

Are these accidental coincidences, or is this the work of someone who intentionally pre-arranged the words to challenge humans? Did these words originate from a prophet, angel, jinn, or human? These verses go against anyone who alleges that the Quran was written by Mohammed. As in mathematics, where there are no disputing results, Allah challenges the critics of His words to picture their claims and compose something as beautiful and complex as the Quran.

CHAPTER 6
HARMONY BETWEEN FAITH AND THE TIME

I am the Time, in My hand is the night and the day.

~Allah

The connection between the Islamic faith and the number of verses contained in the Quran—and how they are mathematically connected to time—is phenomenal. The motive behind this connection is obscure.

Let's look at the following verses that describe a basic principle of the Islamic faith: monotheism.

Daha

(إِنَّنِى أَنَا ٱللَّهُ لَا إِلَٰهَ إِلَّا أَنَا۠ فَٱعْبُدْنِى وَأَقِمِ ٱلصَّلَوٰةَ لِذِكْرِىٓ) (١٤)

«Verily I am Allah: there is no god but I: so, serve thou Me, (only) and establish regular prayer for celebrating My praise. (14)

The verse has twelve words! Does it represent the twelve hours of day or night, or twelve months? Your Lord Is One. Is it a coincidence? No. Is it that Arabic words have a unique rhythm that other languages lack, and therefore, Allah designated it for His last message?

Al Baqarah

(ءَامَنَ ٱلرَّسُولُ بِمَآ أُنزِلَ إِلَيْهِ مِن رَّبِّهِۦ وَٱلْمُؤْمِنُونَۚ كُلٌّ ءَامَنَ بِٱللَّهِ وَمَلَـٰٓئِكَتِهِۦ وَكُتُبِهِۦ وَرُسُلِهِۦ لَا نُفَرِّقُ بَيْنَ أَحَدٍ مِّن رُّسُلِهِۦۚ وَقَالُوا۟ سَمِعْنَا وَأَطَعْنَا غُفْرَانَكَ رَبَّنَا وَإِلَيْكَ ٱلْمَصِيرُ) (٢٨٥)

The Messenger believeth in what hath been revealed to him from his Lord, as do the men of faith. Each one (of them) believeth in Allah, His angels, His books, and His Messengers «We make no distinction (they say) between one and another of His Messengers.» And they say: «We hear and we obey; (We seek) Thy forgiveness, Our Lord, and to Thee is the end of all journeys.» (285)

This verse illustrates four of the six pillars of the Islamic faith. The highlighted pieces are composed of twenty-four words. Muslims know the value of this verse. I won't go deep into its significance and will focus instead on how the Quran conforms with concepts of time, particularly when it emphasis the basic tenet of the Islamic faith, which is monotheism.

Assafaat (Ranged in Row)

(إِنَّ إِلَـٰهَكُمْ لَوَاحِدٌ) (٤)

Verily, verily, your Allah is One! — (4)

This verse outlines the non-negotiable faith (*Iman*) of a real Muslim. Your Lord is One. Only One. It contains just twelve letters, representing hours or months.

Al-Ikhlaas (Fidelity)

قُلْ هُوَ ٱللَّهُ أَحَدٌ (١) ٱللَّهُ ٱلصَّمَدُ (٢) لَمْ يَلِدْ وَلَمْ يُولَدْ (٣) وَلَمْ يَكُن لَّهُۥ كُفُوًا أَحَدٌۢ (٤)

Say: He is Allah, the One! (1) Allah, the eternally Besought of all! (2) He begetteth not nor was begotten. (3) And there is none comparable unto Him. (4)

Look at the highlighted verse; it consists of twelve letters.

This surah is 112th in the Quran. If separated, that number gives one and twelve. Although this surah is like the first part of the shahada, do one and twelve show a secret concept? I assume that the one refers to Allah, and it is an odd number. Twelve, although related to time and an even number, contains two, which reflects the rest of creation.

The surah has just four verses: 1, 2, 3, and 4. Multiplied together, the result is twenty-four (the hours in a day). Why does Allah choose these specific parts of the Quran and relate them with time?

1x2x3x4=24

Al-Imran

شَهِدَ ٱللَّهُ أَنَّهُۥ لَآ إِلَٰهَ إِلَّا هُوَ وَٱلْمَلَٰٓئِكَةُ وَأُو۟لُوا۟ ٱلْعِلْمِ قَآئِمًۢا بِٱلْقِسْطِ لَآ إِلَٰهَ إِلَّا هُوَ ٱلْعَزِيزُ ٱلْحَكِيمُ (١٨)

There is no god but He: that is the witness of Allah His angels and those endued with knowledge, standing firm on justice. There is no god but He, the Exalted in Power, the Wise. (18)

The highlighted portion contains fourteen words, which represent half of a month. Allah says himself that He is the One and the angels testify to that. Building on that, having faith expressed through time-related numbers shows that God wants to remind us of the perfect faith.

Al-Imran

(إِنَّ ٱلَّذِينَ ٱشْتَرَوُاْ ٱلْكُفْرَ بِٱلْإِيمَٰنِ لَن يَضُرُّواْ ٱللَّهَ شَيْـًٔا وَلَهُمْ عَذَابٌ أَلِيمٌ) ١٧٧

Those who purchase disbelief at the price of faith harm Allah not at all, but theirs will be a painful doom. (177)

This verse has a special number, 177, which is exactly half of the days in the lunar year. Its words, numbering fourteen, represent half of the days in a lunar month. Why does this coincidence exist?

Al-Imran

(ٱللَّهُ لَا إِلَٰهَ إِلَّا هُوَ ٱلْحَىُّ ٱلْقَيُّومُ) ٢

Allah! There is no God save Him, the Alive, the Eternal. (2)

This verse contains seven words and twenty-four letters, and there are many similar verses in the Quran. This further backs the idea that Allah is time itself.

Al-Dhariyaat (The Winds)

(وَلَا تَجْعَلُواْ مَعَ ٱللَّهِ إِلَٰهًا ءَاخَرَ إِنِّى لَكُم مِّنْهُ نَذِيرٌ مُّبِينٌ) ٥١

And set not any other god along with Allah; lo! I am a plain warner unto you from Him. (51)

This verse also contains twelve Arabic words. Why does Allah conform verses to time-related numbers when mentioning either Himself or time?

Al-Anbiya (The Prophets)

(وَقَالُوا اتَّخَذَ الرَّحْمَٰنُ وَلَدًا ۗ سُبْحَانَهُ ۚ بَلْ عِبَادٌ مُّكْرَمُونَ ٢٦)

And they say: The Beneficent hath taken unto Himself a son. Be He glorified! Nay, but (those whom they call sons) are honored slaves; (26)

The highlighted section above consists of twenty-four letters if you omit the additional *alif*. The second part, which isn't highlighted, consists of twelve letters. Why is it that these numbers keep showing up when the concept of Allah's exclusiveness is mentioned? The biggest discrepancy between Islam and Christianity, for instance, is mainly that God has a son.

This is a big topic. Although Christianity is one of Abraham's monotheistic religions, there has been a dispute about the nature of Jesus, both in early and current times. As noted in the Oxford Companion to the Bible, "The central tenet of Christianity is the belief in Jesus as the Son of God and the Messiah (Christ). Christians believe that Jesus, as the Messiah, was anointed by God as savior of humanity and hold that Jesus' coming was the fulfillment of messianic prophecies of the Old Testament. The Christian concept of the Messiah differs significantly from the contemporary Jewish concept. The core Christian belief is that through belief in and acceptance of the death and resurrection of Jesus, sinful humans can be reconciled to God and thereby are offered salvation and the promise of eternal life."[5]

In Islam, Jesus (AS) is one of the greatest prophets and the Quran presents this subject as a clear-cut line between real faith

---

5   Metzger/Coogan, *Oxford Companion to the Bible*, pp. 513, 649.

and unreal faith. There is no gray area when the Quran discusses these sensitive subjects.

Al-Qasas (The Stories)

وَلَا تَدْعُ مَعَ ٱللَّهِ إِلَٰهًا ءَاخَرَ لَآ إِلَٰهَ إِلَّا هُوَ كُلُّ شَىْءٍ هَالِكٌ إِلَّا وَجْهَهُ لَهُ ٱلْحُكْمُ وَإِلَيْهِ تُرْجَعُونَ (٨٨)

And cry not unto any other god along with Allah. There is no God save Him. Everything will perish save His countenance. His is the command, and unto Him ye will be brought back. (88)

If you add both the letters from the highlighted portions, you will get thirty-one letters. The first part underlined consists of seven words and confirms the indisputable Oneness of Allah.

Al-Kafirun (The Unbelievers)

قُلْ يَٰٓأَيُّهَا ٱلْكَٰفِرُونَ (١) لَآ أَعْبُدُ مَا تَعْبُدُونَ (٢) وَلَآ أَنتُمْ عَٰبِدُونَ مَآ أَعْبُدُ (٣) وَلَآ أَنَا۠ عَابِدٌ مَّا عَبَدتُّمْ (٤) وَلَآ أَنتُمْ عَٰبِدُونَ مَآ أَعْبُدُ (٥) لَكُمْ دِينُكُمْ وَلِىَ دِينِ (٦)

Say: O ye that reject Faith! (1) I worship not that which ye worship, (2) Nor will ye worship that which I worship. (3) And I will not worship that which ye have been won't to worship, (4) Nor will ye worship that which I worship. (5) To you be your Way, and to me mine. (6)

This short surah is composed of thirty-one words, which represent the days of the month in the solar year. It discusses the freedom of worship. Every person has the right to believe whatever he/she likes and has no obligation to become a Muslim. The Quran is clear on these concepts.

An-Nissaa

(إِنَّ ٱللَّهَ لَا يَغْفِرُ أَن يُشْرَكَ بِهِ وَيَغْفِرُ مَا دُونَ ذَٰلِكَ لِمَن يَشَآءُ وَمَن يُشْرِكْ بِٱللَّهِ فَقَدْ ضَلَّ ضَلَٰلًۢا بَعِيدًا) ١١٦

Allah forgives not (the sin of) joining other gods with Him: but He forgives whom He pleaseth other sins than this: one who joins other gods with Allah, hath strayed far, far away (from the Right). (116)

The highlighted underlined portion has seven words, as does as the non-underlined portion, which could represent the days of a week. Adding both highlighted portions, the sum is fourteen, which shows half the days of February or about all other months. On the other hand, if you group the number of the verse, the result is 12.

(1+1) x 6=12

Al-Imran

(شَهِدَ ٱللَّهُ أَنَّهُۥ لَا إِلَٰهَ إِلَّا هُوَ وَٱلْمَلَٰٓئِكَةُ وَأُو۟لُوا۟ ٱلْعِلْمِ قَآئِمًۢا بِٱلْقِسْطِ لَآ إِلَٰهَ إِلَّا هُوَ ٱلْعَزِيزُ ٱلْحَكِيمُ) ١٨

There is no god but He: that is the witness of Allah His angels and those endued with knowledge, standing firm on justice. There is no god but He, the Exalted in Power, the Wise. (18)

This verse contains seventy-three Arabic letters. The verse number is eighteen. If you multiply the numbers (73x18), the product is 1314. The root of 1314 is 36.25. The surah Al-Imran is third in the Quran. If you subtract one (for Allah) from 36.25, you get 35.25. Divide that by three to get 11.7, which is twelve when rounded.

73x18=1314
√1314=36.25
36.25-1=35.25
35.25/3=11.7~12

Ar-Ra'ad (The Thunder)

(عَٰلِمُ ٱلْغَيْبِ وَٱلشَّهَٰدَةِ ٱلْكَبِيرُ ٱلْمُتَعَالِ ٩)

He knoweth the Unseen and that which is open: He is the Great, the Highest. (9)

This short but great verse has thirty letters, the number of days in a month.

Saad

(قُلْ إِنَّمَآ أَنَا۠ مُنذِرٌۭ وَمَا مِنْ إِلَٰهٍ إِلَّا ٱللَّهُ ٱلْوَٰحِدُ ٱلْقَهَّارُ ٦٥)

Say: «Truly am I a Warner: no god is there but the Allah, the One, Supreme and Irresistible— (65)

This verse contains twelve words, and multiplying its numbers (6x5), the product is 30. How relevant they these numbers?

Daha

(ٱللَّهُ لَآ إِلَٰهَ إِلَّا هُوَ لَهُ ٱلْأَسْمَآءُ ٱلْحُسْنَىٰ ٨)

Allah! there is no god but Him! To Him belong the Most Beautiful Names (8).

This verse has thirty Arabic letters, the days of a month. "This verse shows there is no god but Allah," and its form reflects the concept of time. Therefore, monotheistic faith and the concept of time are compatible with each other.

Ad-Dukhan (Smoke)

(لَا إِلَٰهَ إِلَّا هُوَ يُحْيِي وَيُمِيتُ رَبُّكُمْ وَرَبُّ آبَائِكُمُ الْأَوَّلِينَ) (٨)

There is no god but He: it is He Who gives life and gives death the Lord and Cherisher to you and your earliest ancestors. (8)

This verse contains twelve words, reflecting hours and months. Why is the number twelve regularly balanced with verses that emphasize monotheism? There seems to be a consistent relationship between monotheism and the concept of time.

Allah is eternal, and His words are too, so time is eternal, since He endures. Since the words of the Quran and its structure agree with time, it means it is eternal too.

Daha

(وَإِنِّي لَغَفَّارٌ لِّمَن تَابَ وَآمَنَ وَعَمِلَ صَالِحًا ثُمَّ اهْتَدَىٰ) (٨٢)

«But without doubt, I am (also) He that forgives again, and again to those who repent, believe, and do right— who, in fine, are ready to receive true guidance.» (82)

This verse is composed of twelve words, representing the hours of a day, night, or months of a year.

Al-Shu'ara (The Poets)

(رَبِّ مُوسَىٰ وَهَارُونَ) (٤٨)

«The Lord of Moses and Aaron.» (48)

The verse about the Lord of Moses and Aaron has twelve letters. Amazing! The number of the verse holds time-related numbers too. Forty-eight is the total hours in two days. Divided by two, this gives the hours of one full day. Adding 4 and 8, the sum is 12, day or night.

How can anyone say these arranged Quranic words and letters are accidental or merely manmade?

Al-Ana'am

أَفَغَيْرَ ٱللَّهِ أَبْتَغِى حَكَمًا وَهُوَ ٱلَّذِىٓ أَنزَلَ إِلَيْكُمُ ٱلْكِتَٰبَ مُفَصَّلًا وَٱلَّذِينَ ءَاتَيْنَٰهُمُ ٱلْكِتَٰبَ يَعْلَمُونَ أَنَّهُۥ مُنَزَّلٌ مِّن رَّبِّكَ بِٱلْحَقِّ فَلَا تَكُونَنَّ مِنَ ٱلْمُمْتَرِينَ (١١٤)

Shall I seek other than Allah for judge, when He it is Who hath revealed unto you (this) Scripture, fully explained? Those unto whom We gave the Scripture (aforetime) know that it is revealed from thy Lord in truth. So be not thou (O Muhammad) of the waverers. (114)

There are 114 surahs in the Quran and many speak about the Quran, but what makes this verse special is its number.

No man could have written this with the intention of including these many coincidences.

THE TESTIMONY *(SHAHADA)*

The shahada in Islam has two forms, the first of which is لا إله إلا الله محمد رسول الله. This includes seven words, representing the days in a week. If we split the phrase in half, we get لا إله إلا الله and محمد رسول الله. Each part contains twelve letters, while the letters total twenty-four.

The alternate form is   اشهد ان لا إله إلا الله
واشهد ان محمد رسول الله

This form contains twelve words.

صلى الله على محمد. This phrase has fourteen letters. I will break down the words into letters. The first word contains three letters, the second has four, the third has three, and the final word has four letters. Now we can do some calculations.

3 x 4 = 12
4 x 3 = 12
4+3 = 7
(3 + 3) x 4 = 24
12 + 12 = 24
(4+3) x (4+3) = 31
4 x 4 x 3 x 3 = 144
√144 = 12
144/2 = 72

If you look at the result of the numbers, you will notice they all correspond to a measurement of time. Seventy-two hours is three days.

PROPHET MUHAMMAD (SAW)

The Quran has five locations in its two versions that show the name of the Prophet Mohamad, including the most frequent, Mohammad, and the less frequent, Ahmad. The places noting his name all relate to time. I can't explain why they are encoded this way.

Table 4

Name of Surah	Total verses	Rank	Verse No. has Mohamad	Total words in verse
Al- Imran	200	2	144	30
Al-Ahzaab	73	33	40	20
Muhammad	29	47	2	23
Al-Fathi	48	29	29	30 and 29
Assaf	14	61	6	33
Total		191	221	165

Before I begin the calculations, you will notice in the above table that the highlighted numbers relate closely to time.

Let us discuss this mathematically and play with the numbers. The total number of words in these surahs is 165. Multiplying these numbers (1x6x5), the product is 30, the days of a lunar or solar month. The total of the verse numbers is 221. The root of 221 is 14.866, which, if rounded to 15, is half the days of a month.

The sum of the rank numbers for these suras is 191. Its root is 13.82, and when rounded to 14, is half of a month.

Subtracting 191 from 221 is 30.

Surat Assaf ranks sixty-first in the Quran. If we multiply by six, which is the verse containing Ahmad, it is 366. Subtracting one for Allah from 366, you get 365, the days of the solar year.

Another interesting point is that in the surah Muhammad, the name Muhammad is exactly the twelfth word! Did you notice the number twelve?

I guess that all Muslims know the age of the Prophet Mohammed (SAW), but I can confirm it by playing a mathematical game. If we multiply 165 with 24, which is the hours of a full day, we get 3960. The root of 3960 is 62.9. When rounded to 63, we get the age of the Prophet Muhammad (SAW) when he died.

$1 \times 6 \times 5 = 30$
$\sqrt{221} = 14.866 \sim 15$
$\sqrt{191} = 13.82 \sim 14$
$221 - 191 = 30$
$366 - 1 = 365$
$165 \times 24 = 3960$
$\sqrt{3960} = 62.9 \sim 63$

Al-Munafiqun (The Hypocrities)

وَأَنفِقُوا مِن مَّا رَزَقْنَاكُم مِّن قَبْلِ أَن يَأْتِىَ أَحَدَكُمُ ٱلْمَوْتُ فَيَقُولَ رَبِّ لَوْلَا أَخَّرْتَنِى إِلَىٰ أَجَلٍ قَرِيبٍ فَأَصَّدَّقَ وَأَكُن مِّنَ ٱلصَّٰلِحِينَ (١٠)

And spend of that wherewith We have provided you before death cometh unto one of you and he saith: My Lord! If only thou wouldst reprieve me for a little while, then I would give alms and be among the righteous. (10)

Surah *Al-Munafiqoon* is in the sixty-third place in the Quran, and the Prophet Mohammad's age was 63 at the time of his passing. Is there a correlation between the rank of the surah and the age of the prophet?

Verse 10 relates to time through its twenty-four Arabic words. So, the verse explains how to prepare for the death of any human being, including the prophet Muhammad (SAW). Why are the surah rank and the Prophet's age both 63?

Al-Nasr (Divine Support)

إِذَا جَاءَ نَصْرُ اَللَّهِ وَٱلْفَتْحُ (١) وَرَأَيْتَ ٱلنَّاسَ يَدْخُلُونَ فِى دِينِ ٱللَّهِ أَفْوَاجًا (٢) فَسَبِّحْ بِحَمْدِ رَبِّكَ وَٱسْتَغْفِرْهُ إِنَّهُ كَانَ تَوَّابًا (٣)

When Allah's succor and the triumph cometh (1) And thou seest mankind entering the religion of Allah in troops, (2) Then hymn the praises of thy Lord, and seek forgiveness of Him. Lo! He is ever ready to show mercy. (3)

The majority of Muslim scholars consider this surah the prediction of the Prophet Mohammed's death (SAW). Could there be mathematical evidence to support this?

The surah is short. The three verses are composed of 19, 31, and 30 letters respectively. Obviously, 30 and 31 are the days of both the solar and lunar months.

Multiplied together, the product is 17670. The root of that number is 132.9. If we divide by 2, the result is 66.46. Subtracting 3, which is the number of times Allah and Lord (*Rabbi*) are mentioned, or for the number of verses, the result is 63.46. This is the age of the prophet Muhammad (SAW) when he died on 8 June 632 AD. There might be a few more months than exactly 63 full years.

The date of his death is mathematically related to time!

Surah Mohammad

The surah called Mohammad has special significance because of the name, and as a rule, it reflects concepts of time. It contains thirty-one instances of the names of Allah and Lord, which represents the total days in a solar month.

The most amazing thing in this surah is where the name of Muhammad (SAW) is placed. In the second verse, it is placed in the twelfth position. This time-related number is not a coincidence. It was added deliberately. Why?

CHAPTER 7
HOW TIME IS COMPLEMENTARY TO HUMAN CREATION

THE HUMAN CALENDAR

In the absence of any other proof, the thumb alone would convince me of God›s existence.

- Isaac Newton

The human body is a living calendar. You have seven holes in your body. The first five are in the cranium. The next two are in the end of the digestive tract and the genital area. This represents the days of the week.

There are twelve costal bones in each side of the thoracic cage, which total twenty-four. This represents the hours in a full day. In the cranium, there are twenty-nine individual bones: fifteen facial bones, eight cephalic bones, and six in the middle of both ears. There are exactly thirty-one vertebral bones in the body. The arm is comprised of thirty-one bones in total, including the shoulder. The leg contains thirty bones. The rest of the bones, which are the clavicle (2), sternum (1), pelvic (6), hyoid (1), fabella (2 — 30%

of the human population have this bone) add up to twelve. This represents the hours in each day or night.

The brain is divided into two hemispheres (right and left), and there are twelve pairs of cranial nerves. There are also thirty-one spinal nerves.

The fingers in both hands and feet consist of twelve bones each. If added, both hands have twenty-four, as do both feet. If you add the thumb, there are fourteen in total.

Furthermore, there are twelve organs in your torso. These are the lungs, heart, stomach, spleen, liver, small intestine, large intestine, kidneys, pancreas, urinary bladder, gallbladder, and prostate (males) or uterus (female). If we count all the pairs of bones or organs in our body, we get seven; this excludes the eyes, ears, hands, legs, lungs, kidneys, testes (male), or ovaries (female). Chromosomes are what make every human being on this planet. There are forty-six chromosomes in our bodies. If you multiply 4 by 6, you get 24, which represents the hours in a full day.

In chemistry, we have carbon-12. Why does the most common form of carbon have a time-related number?

The glucose molecule consists of twenty-four atoms. Glucose is the building block for all living components like proteins, lipids, carbohydrates, and nucleic acids. Is there a relationship between time and such a molecule?

TIME-RELATED NUMBERS AND HUMAN CREATION

Many verses describe how Allah created human beings. This includes Adam and the biological evolutions of his children, including the menstrual cycle, spermatogenesis, intrauterine stages, sex differentiation, human development, and death.

The wonder of these verses is how they always conform to the numbers of genetic components of chromosomes, like twenty-three, which is half of forty-six, the total number of human chromosomes. Additionally, they harmonize with the time-related numbers we discussed in previous chapters.

The miracles are the same. Why does Allah choose to relate these numbers with the creation and evolution of human beings? Do these remain a coincidence? No. Is Muhammad a genius mathematician or a great scientist? If he was illiterate (*ummi* in Arabic) and living in an ignorant (*Jahiliyah*) society, where was he getting this accurate knowledge?

Most of these verses explain the creation of human beings and usually focus on the sperm of a male, which is more complicated than a female's ovum. Let's look at some examples.

Al Baqarah

وَإِذْ قَالَ رَبُّكَ لِلْمَلَٰٓئِكَةِ إِنِّى جَاعِلٌ فِى ٱلْأَرْضِ خَلِيفَةً ۖ قَالُوٓا۟ أَتَجْعَلُ فِيهَا مَن يُفْسِدُ فِيهَا وَيَسْفِكُ ٱلدِّمَآءَ وَنَحْنُ نُسَبِّحُ بِحَمْدِكَ وَنُقَدِّسُ لَكَ ۖ قَالَ إِنِّىٓ أَعْلَمُ مَا لَا تَعْلَمُونَ (٣٠)

Behold thy Lord said to the angels: «I will create a vicegerent on earth.» They said «Wilt thou place therein one who will make mischief therein and shed blood? Whilst we do celebrate Thy praises and glorify Thy holy (name)?» He said: «I know what ye know not.» (30)

Why does Allah choose verse 30 for the creation of Adam? There is also a surah named 'Human Being' (*Al insaan*). It includes thirty-one verses and is in chapter 29 of the Quran or Koran. It describes how humans developed from clay to Homo sapiens.

Hold on!

Why is it located in this place and why does it contain this number of verses exactly? It is amazing. Why does Allah connect the creation of humans with words related to time?

Al-Hajj (The Pilgrimage)

يَٰٓأَيُّهَا ٱلنَّاسُ إِن كُنتُمْ فِى رَيْبٍ مِّنَ ٱلْبَعْثِ فَإِنَّا خَلَقْنَٰكُم مِّن تُرَابٍ ثُمَّ مِن نُّطْفَةٍ ثُمَّ مِنْ عَلَقَةٍ ثُمَّ مِن مُّضْغَةٍ مُّخَلَّقَةٍ وَغَيْرِ مُخَلَّقَةٍ لِّنُبَيِّنَ لَكُمْ وَنُقِرُّ فِى ٱلْأَرْحَامِ مَا نَشَآءُ إِلَىٰٓ أَجَلٍ مُّسَمًّى ثُمَّ نُخْرِجُكُمْ طِفْلًا ثُمَّ لِتَبْلُغُوٓا۟ أَشُدَّكُمْ وَمِنكُم مَّن يُتَوَفَّىٰ وَمِنكُم مَّن يُرَدُّ إِلَىٰٓ أَرْذَلِ ٱلْعُمُرِ لِكَيْلَا يَعْلَمَ مِنۢ بَعْدِ عِلْمٍ شَيْـًٔا وَتَرَى ٱلْأَرْضَ هَامِدَةً فَإِذَآ أَنزَلْنَا عَلَيْهَا ٱلْمَآءَ ٱهْتَزَّتْ وَرَبَتْ وَأَنۢبَتَتْ مِن كُلِّ زَوْجٍۭ بَهِيجٍ (٥)

O mankind! If ye are in doubt concerning the Resurrection, then lo! We have created you from dust, then from a drop of seed, then from a clot, then from a little lump of flesh shapely and shapeless, that We may make (it) clear for you. And We cause what We will to remain in the wombs for an appointed time, and afterward We bring you forth as infants, then (give you growth) that ye attain your full strength. And among you there is he who dieth (young), and among you there is he who is brought back to the most abject time of life, so that, after knowledge, he knoweth naught. And thou (Muhammad) sees the earth barren, but when We send down water thereon, it doth thrill and swell and put forth every lovely kind (of growth). (5)

How Time Is Complementary To Human Creation

The highlighted portion describes the details of human development from clay, sperm, through embryo, to fetus, to young adult, old age, and death. It has sixty words. Also, there are twenty-four *alifs*.

Alif in the Arabic language is the first letter that every child learns. It is like "A" in other languages. *Alif* is the beginning of the Arabic alphabet, and this verse describes the beginning of human creation.

Why would it be a coincidence? Did Muhammad (SAW) produce the Quran? Was he a genius mathematician? Absolutely not. If he was unable to read and write, how could he be a talented mathematician? If that's the case, then how did he come up with these precise words? There must be another genius behind this.

Al-Mu'minun (The Believers)

وَلَقَدْ خَلَقْنَا ٱلْإِنسَٰنَ مِن سُلَٰلَةٍ مِّن طِينٍ (١٢) ثُمَّ جَعَلْنَٰهُ نُطْفَةً فِى قَرَارٍ مَّكِينٍ (١٣) ثُمَّ خَلَقْنَا ٱلنُّطْفَةَ عَلَقَةً فَخَلَقْنَا ٱلْعَلَقَةَ مُضْغَةً فَخَلَقْنَا ٱلْمُضْغَةَ عِظَٰمًا فَكَسَوْنَا ٱلْعِظَٰمَ لَحْمًا ثُمَّ أَنشَأْنَٰهُ خَلْقًا ءَاخَرَ ۚ فَتَبَارَكَ ٱللَّهُ أَحْسَنُ ٱلْخَٰلِقِينَ (١٤)

Man We did create from a quintessence (of clay); (12) Then We placed him as (a drop of) sperm in a place of rest firmly fixed; (13) Then We made the sperm into a clot of congealed blood; then of that clot We made a (foetus) lump; then We made out of that lump bones and clothed the bones with flesh; then We developed out of it another creature: so blessed be Allah, the Best to create! (14)

Verses 12, 13, and 14 describe the creation of humans in a precise manner. What is the wisdom behind selecting these numbers for this perfection of human creation?

If you count the highlighted part, there are thirty-one words, reflecting the days of the month in a solar year. Perfect. This surah is ranked twenty-third and has twenty-three uses of the word Rabbi, which is half of the chromosomes contained in one sperm or in one ovum.

After fertilization occurs, there are forty-six human chromosomes. Who organized this perfection?

Back to the math game. If you multiply 12, 13, and 14, the result is 2184. Subtract 60 from 2184 to get 2124. The number sixty, which represents seconds and minutes, comes from adding 23 + 23 + 14, the number of the verse, which is half of one month. Additionally, the root of 2124 is almost 46!

23+23=46
12x13x14=2184
46+14=60
2184-60=2124
√2124=46

At-Tariq (The Morning Star)

فَلْيَنظُرِ ٱلْإِنسَٰنُ مِمَّ خُلِقَ (٥) خُلِقَ مِن مَّآءٍ دَافِقٍ (٦) يَخْرُجُ مِنۢ بَيْنِ ٱلصُّلْبِ وَٱلتَّرَآئِبِ (٧)

Now let man but think from what he is created! (5) He is created from a drop emitted— (6) Proceeding from between the backbone and the ribs: (7)

How Time Is Complementary To Human Creation

The above verses contain fourteen words, which is two weeks (or a half month). Here Allah describes the spermatozoa and ova as the half seed of human creation. The sixth verse has twelve letters. It discusses the ejaculation of semen during the male orgasm. Human sperm live up to twenty-four hours but have a capacity to fertilize for twelve hours.

Half a day is twelve hours, and half the chromosomes in a human being is twenty-three. This is in verse 7. Why the seven in here? Because human fertilization occurs in the second week of the menstruation cycle.

AL-Najm (The Star)

(أَفَرَءَيْتُم مَّا تُمْنُونَ (٥٨

Do ye then see? — The (human seed) that ye throw out, — (58)

What males ejaculate—semen—is their contribution to the new baby. But expressing the amazing fluid into 14 letters (2 weeks or a half month) is marvelous. Half of the human origin comes from sperm!

Al-Kahf

قَالَ لَهُ صَاحِبُهُ وَهُوَ يُحَاوِرُهُ أَكَفَرْتَ بِٱلَّذِى خَلَقَكَ مِن تُرَابٍ ثُمَّ مِن
(نُطْفَةٍ ثُمَّ سَوَّىٰكَ رَجُلًا (٣٧

This verse is number 37. It consists of 17 words and 57 letters. If add these together, the sum is 111. The product of 37 and 57 is 2109. The sum of 2109 and 18, which is the rank of *Kahf*, is 2127. Dividing 2127 by 6, gives 354.5. I think it is clear what this number serves. I can't perceive how mathematics is always superb.

The numerical and time correlations in the Quran

The root of 2109 is approximately 46. ALLAHU AKBAR! "Then Allah fashioned you into man." This means you are carrying 46 chromosomes, 23 from each parent.

Subtracting 111 from 280, which is the length of pregnancy in days, is exactly 169, the number of times Allah is mentioned in surah *Al Tawba*.

37+ 17 +57 =111
37x57 =2109
2109+18 /6=354.5
$\sqrt{2109}$=45.9 means 46 chromosomes
280 days length of pregnancy
280-111=169

Al-Mursalat (The Emissaries)

أَلَمْ نَخْلُقكُّم مِّن مَّآءٍ مَّهِينٍ (٢٠) فَجَعَلْنَٰهُ فِى قَرَارٍ مَّكِينٍ (٢١) إِلَىٰ قَدَرٍ مَّعْلُومٍ (٢٢) فَقَدَرْنَا فَنِعْمَ ٱلْقَٰدِرُونَ (٢٣)

Have We not created you from a fluid (held) despicable? (20) The which We placed in a place of rest, firmly fixed. (21) For a period (of gestation), determined (according to need)? (22) For We do determine (according to need); for We are the Best to determine (things)! (23)

These verses are part of Surat *Al-Mursalat* and talk about the creation of humans from semen. Sperm carries the father's half for his contribution for the coming children. Half, yes. Most of the Quran's expressions that best describe the creation of humans are numbered fourteen or fifteen, which represent half the days of the month.

If you look carefully at these verses, you will notice that the number twenty-three—the number of chromosomes for each of the parents—is apparent.

Who is knowledgeable enough to reveal this information through the Quran? Why are concepts of time associated with the creation of humans?

The following verses each mention sperm and reflect the units of time we commented on earlier. It is the rarity of the Quran that makes is so distinct in literature.

Al-Mursalaat

(أَلَمْ نَخْلُقكُّم مِّن مَّآءٍ مَّهِينٍ) ٢٠

Have We not created you from a fluid (sperm) despicable? (20)

Verse 20 is composed of five words and eighteen letters. Add up these numbers to get twenty-three—half of your existence gifted by your father. Incredible!

5+18=23

Abasa (The Frowned)

(مِن نُّطْفَةٍ خَلَقَهُ ۥ فَقَدَّرَهُ ۥ) ١٩

From a sperm-drop: He hath created him, and then molded him in due proportions; (19)

This verse has fifteen letters, half of the days in a month. Similarly, sperm carries half of your genetic material, contributed by your father.

Yaasiin

(أَوَلَمْ يَرَ ٱلْإِنسَٰنُ أَنَّا خَلَقْنَٰهُ مِن نُّطْفَةٍ فَإِذَا هُوَ خَصِيمٌ مُّبِينٌ ٧٧)

Doth not man see that it is We Who created Him from sperm? Yet behold! He (stands forth) as an open adversary! (77)

There are twelve words in this verse, half of a full day, just as sperm is half of our genetic makeup.

Al-Alaq (The Clot)

(خَلَقَ ٱلْإِنسَٰنَ مِنْ عَلَقٍ ٢)

Created man from a clot. (2)

This verse has the numbered 2 in the surah, which represents day and night and contains 15 letters, half of the days of the month. Multiply with 2 and the result is 30. It is the first surah revealed to the Prophet Mohamed (SAW).

Human beings are composed of 46 chromosomes, which is the double of 23. Doubling 15 is 30.

2x15=30
2x23=46

Al-Hujurat (The Chambers)

يَٰٓأَيُّهَا ٱلنَّاسُ إِنَّا خَلَقْنَٰكُم مِّن ذَكَرٍ وَأُنثَىٰ وَجَعَلْنَٰكُمْ شُعُوبًا وَقَبَآئِلَ لِتَعَارَفُوٓا۟ (إِنَّ أَكْرَمَكُمْ عِندَ ٱللَّهِ أَتْقَىٰكُمْ إِنَّ ٱللَّهَ عَلِيمٌ خَبِيرٌ ١٣)

O mankind! We created you from a single (pair) of a male and a female, and made you into nations and tribes, that ye may know each other (not that ye may despise each other). Verily the most honored of you in the sight of Allah is (he who is)

the most righteous of you. And Allah has full knowledge and is well acquainted (with all things).

The highlighted part contains thirty-one letters and clearly defines the creation of humans from a male and a female. Thirty-one is the days of a solar month, which represents a complete month. Why has Allah expressed the creation of humans in 31 letters?

If you stop at من *(min) from,* the underlined portion, the letters are totaled in 23!

HOW MENSES AND DIVORCE CONFORM TO TIME IN THE QURAN

Al Baqarah

وَيَسْـَٔلُونَكَ عَنِ ٱلْمَحِيضِ ۖ
قُلْ هُوَ أَذًى فَٱعْتَزِلُوا۟ ٱلنِّسَآءَ فِى ٱلْمَحِيضِ ۖ وَلَا تَقْرَبُوهُنَّ حَتَّىٰ يَطْهُرْنَ ۖ فَإِذَا تَطَهَّرْنَ فَأْتُوهُنَّ مِنْ حَيْثُ أَمَرَكُمُ ٱللَّهُ ۚ إِنَّ ٱللَّهَ يُحِبُّ ٱلتَّوَّٰبِينَ وَيُحِبُّ ٱلْمُتَطَهِّرِينَ (٢٢٢)

They ask thee concerning women›s courses. Say: They are a hurt and a pollution; so, keep away from women in their courses, and do not approach them until they are clean. But when they have purified themselves, ye may approach them in any manner, time or place ordained for you by Allah. for Allah loves those who turn to Him constantly and He loves those who keep themselves pure and clean. (222)

The first highlighted portion contains fifteen Arabic letters (without و and). The second section has seven Arabic words. This part describes the damage that can be caused by menstruation. Menses is a seven-day period for most women and Allah chooses seven words to express its duration. The last highlighted section has fourteen words. It is true that women may conceive on the fourteenth day from the first day of menstruation. Also, women contribute half of a person's genetic material, which is expressed in this part as fourteen, which also represents half the days in a month.

What a harmony between the Quran, science, and math! Why is God so accurate scientifically and mathematically?

Another interesting point in this verse is that it has thirty words in total, reflecting the days of one month. If we subtract the number of words, 30, from 222, the number of the verse, the result is 192. The root of 192 is almost 14, the day a woman may became pregnant.

I am excited how Allah is so accurate when He describes such scientific material and how He is so mathematically balanced. The Quran is not simply human words, which are full of imbalances and distorted meanings.

$222 - 30 = 192$

$\sqrt{192} = 13.856 \sim 14$

Al-Talaq (Divorce)

وَٱلَّـٰٓـِٔى يَئِسْنَ مِنَ ٱلْمَحِيضِ مِن نِّسَآئِكُمْ إِنِ ٱرْتَبْتُمْ فَعِدَّتُهُنَّ ثَلَـٰثَةُ أَشْهُرٍ وَٱلَّـٰٓـِٔى لَمْ يَحِضْنَ ۚ وَأُو۟لَـٰتُ ٱلْأَحْمَالِ أَجَلُهُنَّ أَن يَضَعْنَ حَمْلَهُنَّ ۚ وَمَن يَتَّقِ ٱللَّهَ يَجْعَل لَّهُۥ مِنْ أَمْرِهِۦ يُسْرًا (٤) ذَٰلِكَ أَمْرُ ٱللَّهِ أَنزَلَهُۥ إِلَيْكُمْ ۚ وَمَن يَتَّقِ ٱللَّهَ يُكَفِّرْ عَنْهُ سَيِّـَٔاتِهِۦ وَيُعْظِمْ لَهُۥٓ أَجْرًا (٥)

How Time Is Complementary To Human Creation

And for such of your women as despair of menstruation, if ye doubt, their period (of waiting) shall be three months, along with those who have it not. And for those with child, their period shall be till they bring forth their burden. And whosoever keepeth his duty to Allah, He maketh his course easy for him. (4) That is the commandment of Allah which He revealeth unto you. And whoso keepeth his duty to Allah, He will remit from him his evil deeds and magnify reward for him. (5)

Surah *Al-Talaq* is the sixty-fifth surah in the Quran and has twelve verses. 6 x 5 = 30. The highlighted portion of verse 4 contains 12 words and 23 words with underlined portion. God lectures us about menstruation with twenty-three words. What number is this? In most of the menstrual period, women produce one egg in a month. Each ovum contains twenty-three chromosomes. Amazing!

If you add 65, 12 (highlighted portion), and 5, the total is 82. If 82 is divided by 28 (4 weeks), which is the length of the women's cycle, the result is 2.9 (rounded to 3). Three months!

Allah is conscious of the subject discussed in these verses. Wait three months to be sure that the womb is clear of any fetus. Calculated mathematically, three months agrees exactly with the verses.

Women must wait three months before trying to conceive again, and the math agrees with the Quran.

$(65+12+5)/28 = 2.9$ (~3 months)

Al-Baqarah

وَٱلْمُطَلَّقَٰتُ يَتَرَبَّصْنَ بِأَنفُسِهِنَّ ثَلَٰثَةَ قُرُوٓءٍ ۚ وَلَا يَحِلُّ لَهُنَّ أَن يَكْتُمْنَ مَا خَلَقَ ٱللَّهُ فِىٓ أَرْحَامِهِنَّ إِن كُنَّ يُؤْمِنَّ بِٱللَّهِ وَٱلْيَوْمِ ٱلْءَاخِرِ ۚ وَبُعُولَتُهُنَّ أَحَقُّ بِرَدِّهِنَّ فِى ذَٰلِكَ إِنْ أَرَادُوٓا۟ إِصْلَٰحًا ۚ وَلَهُنَّ مِثْلُ ٱلَّذِى عَلَيْهِنَّ بِٱلْمَعْرُوفِ ۚ وَلِلرِّجَالِ عَلَيْهِنَّ دَرَجَةٌ ۗ وَٱللَّهُ عَزِيزٌ حَكِيمٌ (٢٢٨)

Women who are divorced shall wait, keeping themselves apart, three (monthly) courses. And it is not lawful for them that they should conceal that which Allah hath created in their wombs if they are believers in Allah and the Last Day. And their husbands would do better to take them back in that case if they desire a reconciliation. And they (women) have rights like those (of men) over them in kindness, and men are a degree above them. Allah is Mighty, Wise. (228)

The highlighted portion is composed of thirty letters, which represents the days of a full month. Allah is talking about months and his words are balanced with this number. The beauty of this verse is that there are three months with three times repeated in the name of Allah.

If separated, the numbers in the verse (2, 2, and 8) add to make twelve, a time-related number.

An-Nissa

حُرِّمَتْ عَلَيْكُمْ أُمَّهَٰتُكُمْ وَبَنَاتُكُمْ وَأَخَوَٰتُكُمْ وَعَمَّٰتُكُمْ وَخَٰلَٰتُكُمْ وَبَنَاتُ ٱلْأَخِ وَبَنَاتُ ٱلْأُخْتِ وَأُمَّهَٰتُكُمُ ٱلَّٰتِىٓ أَرْضَعْنَكُمْ وَأَخَوَٰتُكُم مِّنَ ٱلرَّضَٰعَةِ وَأُمَّهَٰتُ نِسَآئِكُمْ وَرَبَٰٓئِبُكُمُ ٱلَّٰتِى فِى حُجُورِكُم مِّن نِّسَآئِكُمُ ٱلَّٰتِى دَخَلْتُم بِهِنَّ فَإِن لَّمْ تَكُونُوا۟ دَخَلْتُم بِهِنَّ فَلَا جُنَاحَ عَلَيْكُمْ وَحَلَٰٓئِلُ أَبْنَآئِكُمُ ٱلَّذِينَ مِنْ أَصْلَٰبِكُمْ وَأَن تَجْمَعُوا۟ بَيْنَ ٱلْأُخْتَيْنِ إِلَّا مَا قَدْ سَلَفَ ۗ إِنَّ ٱللَّهَ كَانَ غَفُورًا رَّحِيمًا (٢٣)

Prohibited to you (for marriage) are:— your mothers, daughters, sisters, father›s sisters, mother›s sisters; brother›s daughters, sister›s daughters, foster-mothers (who gave you suck) foster-sisters; your wives› mothers; your step-daughters under your guardianship, born of your wives to whom ye have gone in,—no prohibition if ye have not gone in,— (those who have been) wives of your sons proceeding from your loins; and two sisters in wedlock at one and the same time, except for what is past; for Allah is Oft-Forgiving, Most Merciful. (23)

This verse describes the women you can't marry. Why does this verse carry the number twenty-three? We have seen already that it is the number of chromosomes contributed by women. Aren't you made of forty-six chromosomes? Half from the mother and other half contributed from your father? We originate from a woman, who carries twenty-three chromosomes.

The surah *Al-Nissa* is the fourth in the Quran. In our math game, separating 23 into 2 and 3 then multiplying with 4 (the rank of this surah) the product will be 24.

2x3x4=24

MENSES

Al-Baqarah

وَٱلَّذِينَ يُتَوَفَّوْنَ مِنكُمْ وَيَذَرُونَ أَزْوَاجًا يَتَرَبَّصْنَ بِأَنفُسِهِنَّ أَرْبَعَةَ أَشْهُرٍ وَعَشْرًا فَإِذَا بَلَغْنَ أَجَلَهُنَّ فَلَا جُنَاحَ عَلَيْكُمْ فِيمَا فَعَلْنَ فِىٓ أَنفُسِهِنَّ بِٱلْمَعْرُوفِ وَٱللَّهُ بِمَا تَعْمَلُونَ خَبِيرٌ (٢٣٤)

If any of you die and leave widows behind; they shall wait concerning themselves four months and ten days when they

have fulfilled their term, there is no blame on you if they dispose of themselves in a just and reasonable manner. And Allah is well acquainted with what ye do. (234)

Why are these numbers—2, 3, 4—used in this verse? What is the product of these numbers? Twenty-four, for the hours of one full day. Counting the Arabic words, they are twenty-nine. It speaks about menses with the number of words relating to the number of days in a month! What is this harmony? What is the secret behind this?

In Islamic law, a widowed woman must wait for four months and ten days from the day her husband dies. After that interval, she is legally free to remarry. The wonder of the Quran is how this verse correctly reflects this mathematically.

122 letters.
122/29 = 4.2
4 months and 2 weeks
2 weeks =14 days
14 – 4 = 10 days.
The number four comes from the verse (four months)
4 months and 10 days. Amazing!
The number of this verse is 234, and 2x3x4=24 hours of a full day!

Al-Baqarah

وَٱلَّذِينَ يُتَوَفَّوْنَ مِنكُمْ وَيَذَرُونَ أَزْوَاجًا وَصِيَّةً لِّأَزْوَاجِهِم مَّتَٰعًا إِلَى ٱلْحَوْلِ غَيْرَ إِخْرَاجٍ فَإِنْ خَرَجْنَ فَلَا جُنَاحَ عَلَيْكُمْ فِى مَا فَعَلْنَ فِىٓ أَنفُسِهِنَّ مِن مَّعْرُوفٍ وَٱللَّهُ عَزِيزٌ حَكِيمٌ (٢٤٠)

(In the case of) those of you who are about to die and leave behind them wives, they should bequeath unto their wives a

How Time Is Complementary To Human Creation

provision for the year without turning them out, but if they go out (of their own accord) there is no sin for you in that which they do of themselves within their rights. Allah is Mighty, Wise. (240)

This verse describes the duration of grieving for a widow, and how to be well-treated, which is up to one year. The number of the verse is 240(24+0), which represents the hours of a full day. If subtracted from 354, which is the days of the lunar year, the result is 114. That is the total number of surahs in the Noble Quran. The verse contains thirty words, which represents the days of one lunar or solar month. Adding 240 to 30, the sum is 270. Dividing 270 by 30 is 9, which is the number of months in a pregnancy. If you add 24 with zero, the result is 24. 30 can be separated as 3 and 0 and sum is 3.

Count the Arabic words; it is stunning. There are thirty words. Who can arrange this with such artistic harmony?

24+0=24
345-240=114
240+30=270
270/30=9
(3+0) =3
9+3=12

****

What is making Koran scientifically miracle is how all phenomenon related to the human evolution represent to time-related numbers. For instance, menses, sperm and in general embryology. I don't have any concept why Allah joins all these biological events to the time-related numbers.

CHAPTER 8
THE CREATION OF JESUS

HOW MANY CHROMOSOMES DID JESUS HAVE?

This kind of question may be disturbing to some people. I am aware of the sensitivity of Muslims and non-Muslims, which can make such a topic difficult. Discussing the most controversial topics is not forbidden religiously and ethically. I am confident that the more someone asks questions, the more he gets the right answers. In this book, I am looking for answers about many confusing inquiries, and I have become comfortable with the topic. I am not a fan of the idea of being a bowl that accepts any kind of food. The freedom of thinking is the most valuable gift delivered by God.

I have spent many years thinking and looking for acceptable interpretations for many topics, including the idea of the root of Jesus (*Issa*, AS). I looked thoroughly through the Quran to discover how it refers to Jesus mathematically.

The complicated question is this: if Jesus is the son of God, does God carry any human DNA?

The Creation Of Jesus

Let's look at how the Quran conforms with the creation of Jesus using plain mathematics.

Al-Imran

إِنَّ مَثَلَ عِيسَىٰ عِندَ ٱللَّهِ كَمَثَلِ ءَادَمَ ۖ خَلَقَهُۥ مِن تُرَابٍ ثُمَّ قَالَ لَهُۥ كُن فَيَكُونُ (٥٩)

This similitude of Jesus before Allah is as that of Adam: He created him from dust, then said to him: «Be» and he was. (59)

This verse compares the creation of Adam and Jesus (AS). It consists of fifteen Arabic words. Fifteen is half of a month and this may mean that God created Jesus from half of the parental material, as well as Adam. Didn't Mary have twenty-three chromosomes? That was half of what was needed to make Jesus, and yet he was born.

Well, look at the number of the verse. Doesn't 5 + 9 = 14? It is an excellent choice.

Why are two people without a father and mother, like Adam, and one without an earthly father, like Jesus, expressed using half numbers related to time? What is the similarity they share in the first place?

Phenomena like this, which agrees scientifically and mathematically with the Quran, are something rare.

Al-Imran

إِذْ قَالَتِ ٱلْمَلَٰٓئِكَةُ يَٰمَرْيَمُ إِنَّ ٱللَّهَ يُبَشِّرُكِ بِكَلِمَةٍ مِّنْهُ ٱسْمُهُ ٱلْمَسِيحُ عِيسَى ٱبْنُ مَرْيَمَ وَجِيهًا فِى ٱلدُّنْيَا وَٱلْءَاخِرَةِ وَمِنَ ٱلْمُقَرَّبِينَ (٤٥)

(And remember) when the angels said: O Mary! Lo! Allah giveth thee glad tidings of a word from him, whose name is

the Messiah, Jesus, son of Mary, illustrious in the world and the Hereafter, and one of those brought near (unto Allah).

Verse 45 shows the giving of the word (Jesus) to Mary. A human usually has forty-six chromosomes, while in the creation of Jesus, Allah chose forty-five as the verse number. Did Jesus lack one Y chromosome? The concept in this verse—the creation of Jesus from a woman who had no sexual contact with a man—is encoded in the right place in the Quran. Why 45?

Al-Imran

قَالَتْ رَبِّ أَنَّىٰ يَكُونُ لِى وَلَدٌ وَلَمْ يَمْسَسْنِى بَشَرٌ ۖ قَالَ كَذَٰلِكِ ٱللَّهُ يَخْلُقُ مَا يَشَآءُ ۚ إِذَا قَضَىٰٓ أَمْرًا فَإِنَّمَا يَقُولُ لَهُۥ كُن فَيَكُونُ (٤٧)

She said: My Lord! How can I have a child when no mortal hath touched me? He said: So (it will be). Allah creates what He will. If He decree a thing, He saith unto it only: Be! and it is. (47)

You will be just as surprised about this verse as I was when I first manipulated it mathematically. It is number forty-seven and has twenty-four words. Here, the creation of Jesus may also be related to time.

Everything is confirmed in this verse, but what makes it exciting is how it reflects half of the chromosomes of a human being. Subtracting the number of words, 24, from the verse number, 47, gives you 23.

I am confident that this type of coding could not be written by humans. It reflects superb intelligence. These details were selected carefully and arranged in a manner distinct from any authors in human history.

The Creation Of Jesus

Look at the highlighted word(creates) is in the fourteenth place of the verse.

47-24=23

Al-Maeda

لَقَدْ كَفَرَ ٱلَّذِينَ قَالُوٓاْ إِنَّ ٱللَّهَ هُوَ ٱلْمَسِيحُ ٱبْنُ مَرْيَمَۖ وَقَالَ ٱلْمَسِيحُ يَٰبَنِىٓ إِسْرَٰٓءِيلَ ٱعْبُدُواْ ٱللَّهَ رَبِّى وَرَبَّكُمْۖ إِنَّهُۥ مَن يُشْرِكْ بِٱللَّهِ فَقَدْ حَرَّمَ ٱللَّهُ عَلَيْهِ ٱلْجَنَّةَ وَمَأْوَىٰهُ ٱلنَّارُۖ وَمَا لِلظَّٰلِمِينَ مِنْ أَنصَارٍ (٧٢)

They surely disbelieve who say: Lo! Allah is the Messiah, son of Mary. The Messiah (himself) said: O Children of Israel, worship Allah, my Lord and your Lord. Lo! whoso ascribes partners unto Allah, for him Allah hath forbidden paradise. His abode is the Fire. For evil doers, there will be no helpers. (72)

Multiplying 7 by 2, the result is 14—half of the days in a month. Jesus was created from half the normal number of parents! He originated from Mary. Only Mary. The Virgin Mary.

Let us go deep into this calculation to prove that Jesus had only twenty-three chromosomes, according to many verses in the Quran.

This verse contains thirty-seven Arabic words. 37 − 14 = 23! Amazing! Where there is the name of Jesus, son of Mary, there will be the numbers 23 or 45!

What is the rationale behind this?

7x2=14
37-14=23

Al-Maida

إِذْ قَالَ اللَّهُ يَٰعِيسَى ابْنَ مَرْيَمَ اذْكُرْ نِعْمَتِى عَلَيْكَ وَعَلَىٰ وَٰلِدَتِكَ إِذْ أَيَّدتُّكَ بِرُوحِ الْقُدُسِ تُكَلِّمُ النَّاسَ فِى الْمَهْدِ وَكَهْلًا ۖ وَإِذْ عَلَّمْتُكَ الْكِتَٰبَ وَالْحِكْمَةَ وَالتَّوْرَىٰةَ وَالْإِنجِيلَ ۖ وَإِذْ تَخْلُقُ مِنَ الطِّينِ كَهَيْـَٔةِ الطَّيْرِ بِإِذْنِى فَتَنفُخُ فِيهَا فَتَكُونُ طَيْرًۢا بِإِذْنِى ۖ وَتُبْرِئُ الْأَكْمَهَ وَالْأَبْرَصَ بِإِذْنِى ۖ وَإِذْ تُخْرِجُ الْمَوْتَىٰ بِإِذْنِى ۖ وَإِذْ كَفَفْتُ بَنِىٓ إِسْرَٰٓءِيلَ عَنكَ إِذْ جِئْتَهُم بِالْبَيِّنَٰتِ فَقَالَ الَّذِينَ كَفَرُواْ مِنْهُمْ إِنْ هَٰذَآ إِلَّا سِحْرٌ مُّبِينٌ (١١٠)

When Allah saith: O Jesus, son of Mary! Remember My favor unto thee and unto thy mother; how I strengthened thee with the holy Spirit, so that thou spakest unto mankind in the cradle as in maturity; and how I taught thee the Scripture and Wisdom and the Torah and the Gospel; and how thou didst shape of clay as it were the likeness of a bird by My permission, and didst blow upon it and it was a bird by My permission, and thou didst heal him who was born blind and the leper by My permission; and how thou didst raise the dead by My permission; and how I restrained the Children of Israel from (harming) thee when thou camest unto them with clear proofs, and those of them who disbelieved exclaimed: This is naught else than evident magic; (110)

This verse is on page 126. Multiplying 1, 2, and 6 produces 12. The verse contains seventy-four words. Multiply 74 with 12 to get 888. The root of 888 is about 30. Subtracting 30 from 74 will be 44. This verse contains one instance of the name Allah. Adding 44 with 1, the sum is 45. Is this the total number of chromosomes of Jesus?

Was the forty-sixth chromosome missing? Is it the Y chromosome?

8+8+8=24
1x2x6=12
74x12=888
√888=29.799 ~ 30
74-30=44
44+1=45

Al-Maida

إِذْ قَالَ ٱلْحَوَارِيُّونَ يَٰعِيسَى ٱبْنَ مَرْيَمَ هَلْ يَسْتَطِيعُ رَبُّكَ أَن يُنَزِّلَ عَلَيْنَا مَآئِدَةً مِّنَ ٱلسَّمَآءِ قَالَ ٱتَّقُوا۟ ٱللَّهَ إِن كُنتُم مُّؤْمِنِينَ (١١٢)

When the disciples said: O Jesus, son of Mary! Is thy Lord able to send down for us a table spread with food from heaven? He said: Observe your duty to Allah, if ye are true believers. (112)

This verse contains the name of Jesus, son of Mary. If you separate 112 as 1 and 12, the product is 12. That is related to time.

There are twenty-one words in this verse and it uses Allah and *Rabbi* (Lord) once each. Adding twenty-one with two names gives twenty-three. This occurrence of the number twenty-three is remarkable.

Why does this number occur? I guess that the birth of Jesus (AS) is a miracle and He may have had twenty-three or forty-five chromosomes.

1x12=12
21 words
21+2=23

Maryam (Mary)

فَأَجَاءَهَا ٱلْمَخَاضُ إِلَىٰ جِذْعِ ٱلنَّخْلَةِ قَالَتْ يَٰلَيْتَنِى مِتُّ قَبْلَ هَٰذَا وَكُنتُ نَسْيًا مَّنسِيًّا (٢٣)

And the pangs of childbirth drove her unto the trunk of the palm-tree. She said: Oh, would that I had died ere this and had become a thing of naught, forgotten! (23)

The miracle of miracles. The day that Mary got the pain of labor to give birth to Jesus (AS) is described in the twenty-third verse in the Quran. What is going on?

Isn't twenty-three the number of chromosomes in the gametes of both females and males? Didn't Jesus come from only a single woman, Mary? Stunning!

In Arabic, there are fourteen words, half of a month. There are fifty-six letters. Multiply 5 with 6 to get 30.

(ذَٰلِكَ عِيسَى ٱبْنُ مَرْيَمَ قَوْلَ ٱلْحَقِّ ٱلَّذِى فِيهِ يَمْتَرُونَ) ٣٤

Such was Jesus, son of Mary: (this is) a statement of the truth concerning which they doubt. (34)

Separating 34 into 3 and 4, will result is 12 when multiplied. The highlighted piece of this verse has fifteen letters—half of the days in one month. The page containing this verse has two uses of the name Allah and one *Lillah*. Allah is composed in Arabic of four letters, where *Lillah* has just three letters. Multiplying 4 by 2 is 8 and adding 3 is 11. Subtracting 11 from 34 is 23. Half of Mary's chromosomes, which she passed onto Jesus.

The Creation Of Jesus

3x4=12
8+3=11
34-11=23

قَالَ إِنِّى عَبْدُ ٱللَّهِ ءَاتَىٰنِىَ ٱلْكِتَٰبَ وَجَعَلَنِى نَبِيًّا (٣٠) وَجَعَلَنِى مُبَارَكًا أَيْنَ مَا كُنتُ وَأَوْصَىٰنِى بِٱلصَّلَوٰةِ وَٱلزَّكَوٰةِ مَا دُمْتُ حَيًّا (٣١)

He said: Lo! I am the slave of Allah. He hath given me the Scripture and hath appointed me a Prophet, (30) And hath made me blessed wheresoever I may be, and hath enjoined upon me prayer and almsgiving so long as I remain alive, (31)

These two verses contain nine and fourteen words, respectively. Adding both numbers, we get twenty-three. The numbers of both verses correspond to the days in a month, whether lunar or solar—30 and 31. And 23 corresponds the DNA of gametes in this case for Mary.

9+14= 23

As-Saff (The Ranks)

وَإِذْ قَالَ عِيسَى ٱبْنُ مَرْيَمَ يَٰبَنِىٓ إِسْرَٰٓءِيلَ إِنِّى رَسُولُ ٱللَّهِ إِلَيْكُم مُّصَدِّقًا لِّمَا بَيْنَ يَدَىَّ مِنَ ٱلتَّوْرَىٰةِ وَمُبَشِّرًۢا بِرَسُولٍ يَأْتِى مِنۢ بَعْدِى ٱسْمُهُۥٓ أَحْمَدُ ۖ فَلَمَّا جَآءَهُم بِٱلْبَيِّنَٰتِ قَالُوا۟ هَٰذَا سِحْرٌ مُّبِينٌ (٦)

And when Jesus son of Mary said: O Children of Israel! Lo! I am the messenger of Allah unto you, confirming that which was (revealed) before me in the Torah, and bringing good tidings of a messenger who cometh after me, whose name is the Praised One. Yet when he hath come unto them with clear proofs, they say: This is mere magic. (6)

This verse number is six (half of twelve) and it contains thirty-three words. The page number of this surah is 552. If 33 is subtracted from 522, it gives 519. The root of this number, if rounded, is 23!

12/2=6
552-33=519
√519=22.78~23

Assaf

يَـٰٓأَيُّهَا ٱلَّذِينَ ءَامَنُوا۟ كُونُوٓا۟ أَنصَارَ ٱللَّهِ كَمَا قَالَ عِيسَى ٱبْنُ مَرْيَمَ لِلْحَوَارِيِّـۧنَ مَنْ أَنصَارِىٓ إِلَى ٱللَّهِ ۖ قَالَ ٱلْحَوَارِيُّونَ نَحْنُ أَنصَارُ ٱللَّهِ ۖ فَـَٔامَنَت طَّآئِفَةٌ مِّنۢ بَنِىٓ إِسْرَٰٓءِيلَ وَكَفَرَت طَّآئِفَةٌ ۖ فَأَيَّدْنَا ٱلَّذِينَ ءَامَنُوا۟ عَلَىٰ عَدُوِّهِمْ فَأَصْبَحُوا۟ ظَـٰهِرِينَ (١٤)

Ye who believe! Be Allah›s helpers, even as Jesus son of Mary said unto the disciples: Who are my helpers for Allah? They said: We are Allah›s helpers. And a party of the Children of Israel believed, while a party disbelieved. Then We strengthened those who believed against their foe, and they became the uppermost. (14)

This verse's number is fourteen—half of the days in a lunar or solar month. Jesus originated from half of the chromosomes that belonged to his mother.

This verse has thirty-seven Arabic words. So, 37-14 = 23—half of the chromosomes in humans.

On the other hand, this surah uses the name Allah four times. In Arabic, Allah is composed of four letters. Four by four is sixteen. Adding this to fourteen gives thirty.

Subtracting 30 from 552 (the page number) gives 522. The root of 522 is 22.8, rounded to 23.

34-14=23
16+14=30
552-30=522
√522=22.8~23

At-Tahrim (The Banning)

وَمَرْيَمَ ٱبْنَتَ عِمْرَٰنَ ٱلَّتِىٓ أَحْصَنَتْ فَرْجَهَا فَنَفَخْنَا فِيهِ مِن رُّوحِنَا وَصَدَّقَتْ بِكَلِمَٰتِ رَبِّهَا وَكُتُبِهِۦ وَكَانَتْ مِنَ ٱلْقَٰنِتِينَ (١٢)

And Mary, daughter of ‹Imran, whose body was chaste, therefor We breathed therein something of Our Spirit. And she put faith in the words of her Lord and His scriptures, and was of the obedient. (12)

This verse is twelfth. I loved this number. There are twenty-one Arabic words in this verse. Allah is used five times and Lord (*Rabbi*) four times in this surah, which is nine in total. Adding twenty-one with nine gives thirty.

Allah has four letters in Arabic (5x4=20) and Lord (*Rabbi*) fourteen letters. The total number of letters in Allah and Lord is thirty-four. Divide 34 by 2 to get 17. Adding 17 and 5 gives 22. Adding 22 with1-her Lord (*Rabbiha*), the sum is 23. It is really 23!

21+9=30
34/2=17
17+5+1=23

Az-Zukhruf (Ornaments of Gold)

(وَلَمَّا ضُرِبَ ٱبْنُ مَرْيَمَ مَثَلًا إِذَا قَوْمُكَ مِنْهُ يَصِدُّونَ) (٥٧)

And when the son of Mary is quoted as an example, behold! the folk laugh out, (57)

This verse has ten words and thirty-three letters. Subtracting ten from thirty-three is twenty-three.

I can't explain how the number twenty-three comes up so frequently in most verses about Jesus. Isn't the Quran a miracle?

Az-Zukhruf

(إِنَّ ٱللَّهَ هُوَ رَبِّي وَرَبُّكُمْ فَٱعْبُدُوهُ هَٰذَا صِرَاطٌ مُسْتَقِيمٌ) (٦٤)

Lo! Allah, He is my Lord and your Lord. So, worship Him. This is a right path. (64)

If you ponder the highlighted portion, you will see it consists of twenty-three Arabic letters. What is going on? Do these verses prove that Jesus had twenty-three chromosomes? Why are these numbers accurately encoded in the Quran? Who wrote it?

This is what Jesus declared before: "Worship Allah."

The number of the verse itself is not random because if separated and multiplied, it is twenty-four, which is a time-related number. I am persuaded that no human could write a book like the Quran.

Al-Tawba

ٱتَّخَذُوٓا۟ أَحْبَارَهُمْ وَرُهْبَٰنَهُمْ أَرْبَابًا مِّن دُونِ ٱللَّهِ وَٱلْمَسِيحَ ٱبْنَ مَرْيَمَ وَمَآ أُمِرُوٓا۟ (إِلَّا لِيَعْبُدُوٓا۟ إِلَٰهًا وَٰحِدًا ۖ لَّآ إِلَٰهَ إِلَّا هُوَ ۚ سُبْحَٰنَهُۥ عَمَّا يُشْرِكُونَ) (٣١)

The Creation Of Jesus

They have taken as lords beside Allah their rabbis and their monks and the Messiah son of Mary, when they were bidden to worship only One God. There is no god save Him. Be He glorified from all that they ascribe as partner (unto Him)! (31)

This verse is composed of twenty-six words. It has three versions of the name of Allah (three times). If three is subtracted from twenty-six, we get twenty-three. The number of this verse is thirty-one, a time-related number.

HOW OLD WAS JESUS?

Maryam

(وَٱلسَّلَٰمُ عَلَىَّ يَوْمَ وُلِدتُّ وَيَوْمَ أَمُوتُ وَيَوْمَ أُبْعَثُ حَيًّا ٣٣)

Peace on me the day I was born, and the day I die, and the day I shall be raised alive! (33)

Most Christians and Muslims believe Jesus was thirty-three years old when he died. Is there any proof in the Quran? Yes.Maryam

In the thirty-third verse of Surat Maryam. Jesus said, «The day I was born and the day I die. » Why does Allah adopt this number (33)? What is the motive behind choosing this number for the life span of Jesus (AS)? Was Allah saying, "Hi Jesus, you are originated from Mary, who carried 23 chromosomes, and here are the mathematical clues?"

In Surat Maryam, Allah is mentioned eight times, Lord (*Rabbi*) twenty-three times, and Rahman sixteen times. What do these numbers indicate? Christians use the word Lord more often than Muslims. Why is Lord used in this surah exactly twenty-three times? What is behind this? Could it be here accidently, or it is coded intentionally?

Another surprise is that the other two numbers have a mathematical relationship. Eight (the number of times Allah is mentioned) is half of sixteen. Why half? Why are Jesus and the number twenty-three (half of human chromosomes) so connected? Who buried these sophisticated secret numbers in this book?

DEATH, AGING, AND TIME

The following three verses were selected by Allah to discuss the end of life for living organisms. They are all composed of fifteen letters, half of a month. Do living organisms have one full life, half before death and half after? The answer from most religions is yes.

Look how the Quran interacts mathematically with the concept of death, as shown through time-related numbers.

Al-Imran

(كُلُّ نَفْسٍ ذَآئِقَةُ ٱلْمَوْتِ) (١٨٥)

Every soul will taste of death. (185)

Al-Anbiyaa

(كُلُّ نَفْسٍ ذَآئِقَةُ ٱلْمَوْتِ) (٣٥)

Every soul will taste of death. (35)

Surah *Al-Imran* is third and surah *Al-Anbiya* is twenty-first in the Quran. If you add these together, you get twenty-four, which

Al-Ankaboot

(كُلُّ نَفْسٍ ذَآئِقَةُ ٱلْمَوْتِ ثُمَّ إِلَيْنَا تُرْجَعُونَ ٥٧)

Every soul will taste of death. Then unto Us ye will be returned. (57)

Surah *Al-Ankaboot* (The Spider) is twenty-ninth in the Quran, which represents the days of a lunar month. In verse 57, Allah carefully chose seven words in Arabic to reflect the days of one week. The verse number is fifty-seven, which when added is twelve.

The question is, why did Allah select these time-related numbers for a position where He explains death?

The miracles do not stop there. The page number for this verse is 403. Subtracting 57 from 403 is 346. Add that with six, which is the number of times Allah is mentioned, to get 352. There are one Lord (*Rabbi*) and one He. If these two are added with 352, the sum is 354, the days of the lunar year. On this page, Allah is talking about the day, the sun, and the moon.

5+7=12
403-57=346
356+6=352
352+2=354

Yasin

(وَمَن نُّعَمِّرْهُ نُنَكِّسْهُ فِى ٱلْخَلْقِ أَفَلَا يَعْقِلُونَ ٦٨)

If We grant long life to any, We cause him to be reversed in nature: will they not then understand? (68)

Describing the aging process in humans with thirty words is a miracle. The above verse is composed of thirty letters in Arabic. Month after month, we feel the progress of aging.

Al-Anaam

(وَهُوَ ٱلَّذِى يَتَوَفَّىٰكُم بِٱلَّيْلِ وَيَعْلَمُ مَا جَرَحْتُم بِٱلنَّهَارِ ثُمَّ يَبْعَثُكُمْ فِيهِ لِيُقْضَىٰٓ أَجَلٌ مُّسَمًّى ثُمَّ إِلَيْهِ مَرْجِعُكُمْ ثُمَّ يُنَبِّئُكُم بِمَا كُنتُمْ تَعْمَلُونَ) ٦٠

It is He Who doth take your souls by night and hath knowledge of all that ye have done by day; by day doth He raise you up again; that a term appointed be fulfilled; in the end unto Him will be your return then will He show you the truth of all that ye did. (60)

This verse contains twenty-four words and its number is sixty. It says, *"I know what you are doing second by second."* Is Allah choosing to express how closely He monitors us day and night through the number sixty? Very strange!

Al-Hijr

(لَعَمْرُكَ إِنَّهُمْ لَفِى سَكْرَتِهِمْ يَعْمَهُونَ) ٧٢

By thy life (O Muhammad) they moved blindly in the frenzy of approaching death. (72)

This verse has twenty-four letters. The number of the verse itself is seventy-two. This represents three days. The rank of Surah *Hijr* is fifteenth, which represents half of a month.

The Creation Of Jesus

Why does Allah swear on Prophet Muhammad›s (SAW) life in this verse with a time-related number? Why is it that these miraculous correlations occur when Allah is speaking about an aspect of time?

****

Discussing Jesus (AS), his mother, and human creation typically produces many disputes from both religion and science. In my believe the Quran must be accurate mathematically about this argument. Chromosomes were discovered in the 1920s by Theophilus Painter, and DNA in the 1960s by Watson and Crick. The Quran is more than fourteen centuries old and uses 23, 46, and time-related number accurately to reflect what we only learned in the last century. Did God bury these coded ideas in obscure numbers? Why is He so accurate when talking about Jesus (AS) and human creation in general, and why does he associate it with the subject of time?

A large portion of the Quran relates to time, and this confirms the credibility of this sacred text.

CHAPTER 9
MISCELLANEOUS VERSES RELEVANT TO TIME

The following verses are examples of time-related subjects but the concepts they define are not related to each other. I discuss them to show how the Quran reflects time despite disparate meanings.

An-Nissa

$$\text{أَفَلَا يَتَدَبَّرُونَ ٱلْقُرْءَانَ ۚ وَلَوْ كَانَ مِنْ عِندِ غَيْرِ ٱللَّهِ لَوَجَدُوا۟ فِيهِ ٱخْتِلَٰفًا كَثِيرًا} \text{ (٨٢)}$$

Do they not ponder on the Qur'an (with care)? Had it been from other than Allah, they would surely have found therein much discrepancy. (82)

This verse contains fourteen or fifteen words. I do not know what to say after this. The infallibility of God and the Quran is reflected in this verse. If the Quran was generated by humans or someone other than God, we would have detected countless mistakes. It would be mathematically distorted and scientifically phony.

Miscellaneous Verses Relevant To Time

Al-Imran

إِذْ تَقُولُ لِلْمُؤْمِنِينَ أَلَن يَكْفِيَكُمْ أَن يُمِدَّكُمْ رَبُّكُم بِثَلَٰثَةِ ءَالَٰفٍ مِّنَ ٱلْمَلَٰٓئِكَةِ مُنزَلِينَ (١٢٤)

Remember thou saidst to the Faithful: Is it not enough for you that Allah should help you with three thousand angels (specially) sent down? (124)

This verse contains a special number, 3000, and has thirteen words. If 13 is subtracted from 3000 and then divided by 124, the number of the verse, the result is twenty-four.

3000-13/124=24

Al-Imran

بَلَىٰٓ إِن تَصْبِرُواْ وَتَتَّقُواْ وَيَأْتُوكُم مِّن فَوْرِهِمْ هَٰذَا يُمْدِدْكُمْ رَبُّكُم بِخَمْسَةِ ءَالَٰفٍ مِّنَ ٱلْمَلَٰٓئِكَةِ مُسَوِّمِينَ (١٢٥)

«Yea»— if ye remain firm, and act aright, even if the enemy should rush here on you in hot haste, your Lord would help you with five thousand angels making a terrific onslaught. (125)

In this verse, Allah mentions five thousand angels. If this is divided by the number of words in the verse-seventeen and added to sixty—originated from 125 (12 x 5)—the result is 354, which is the days of a lunar year.

12x5=60
(5000/17) +60=354

Al-Imran

وَمَا مُحَمَّدٌ إِلَّا رَسُولٌ قَدْ خَلَتْ مِن قَبْلِهِ ٱلرُّسُلُ أَفَإِيْن مَّاتَ أَوْ قُتِلَ ٱنقَلَبْتُمْ عَلَىٰ أَعْقَابِكُمْ وَمَن يَنقَلِبْ عَلَىٰ عَقِبَيْهِ فَلَن يَضُرَّ ٱللَّهَ شَيْئًا وَسَيَجْزِى ٱللَّهُ ٱلشَّاكِرِينَ (١٤٤)

Muhammad is no more than a Messenger: many were the Messengers that passed away before Him. If he died or was slain, will ye then turn back on your heels? If any did turn back on his heels, not the least harm will he do to Allah; but Allah (on the other hand) will swiftly reward those who (serve him) with gratitude. (144)

This is verse 144. This number, if rooted, is twelve, a time-related number. Furthermore, there are thirty words in this verse!

The verse explains that Mohammad is just a messenger and died as other humans, so the religion is not related to his death and the Quran will be eternal, as Allah is immortal. This is related directly with 144, a time-related number.

أعوذ بالله من الشيطان الرجيم

I seek refuge with Allah from the accursed Satan.

The Arabic language is strange. Consider that this prominent sentence is composed of twenty-four letters. Why? Satan is busy twenty-four hours a day!

NUMBER 40

Axqaaf (The Wind-Curved Sandhills)

Miscellaneous Verses Relevant To Time

وَوَصَّيْنَا ٱلْإِنسَٰنَ بِوَٰلِدَيْهِ إِحْسَٰنًا حَمَلَتْهُ أُمُّهُ كُرْهًا وَوَضَعَتْهُ كُرْهًا وَحَمْلُهُ وَفِصَٰلُهُ ثَلَٰثُونَ شَهْرًا حَتَّىٰٓ إِذَا بَلَغَ أَشُدَّهُ وَبَلَغَ أَرْبَعِينَ سَنَةً قَالَ رَبِّ أَوْزِعْنِىٓ أَنْ أَشْكُرَ نِعْمَتَكَ ٱلَّتِىٓ أَنْعَمْتَ عَلَىَّ وَعَلَىٰ وَٰلِدَىَّ وَأَنْ أَعْمَلَ صَٰلِحًا تَرْضَىٰهُ وَأَصْلِحْ لِى فِى ذُرِّيَّتِىٓ إِنِّى تُبْتُ إِلَيْكَ وَإِنِّى مِنَ ٱلْمُسْلِمِينَ (١٥)

We have enjoined on man Kindness to his parents: in pain did his mother bear him, and in pain did she give him birth. The carrying of the (child) to his weaning is (a period of) thirty months. At length, when he reaches the age of full strength and attains forty years, he says «O my Lord! Grant me that I may be grateful for Thy favor which Thou hast bestowed upon me, and upon both my parents, and that I may work righteousness such as Thou mayest approve; and be gracious to me in my issue. Truly have I turned to Thee and truly do I bow (to Thee) in Islam.» (15)

In this verse, Allah illustrates the best age of man, which is forty years. Forty years is 480 months. If added to 30 months, which is the weaning period of a child, the sum is 510. If 510 is divided by two, which comes from the division of 30 by 15 (the number of the verse), the result is 2. Divide 510 by 2 and the result is 255. Subtract 255 from 354, which is the days of lunar year, to get 99, which is the names of Allah. Add 99 with 15, the sum is 114, which is the number of surahs in the Quran.

40x12=480
480+30=510
30/15=2
510/2=255
354-255=99
99+15=114

Al-Maeda (*The Table*)

قَالَ فَإِنَّهَا مُحَرَّمَةٌ عَلَيْهِمْ أَرْبَعِينَ سَنَةً يَتِيهُونَ فِى ٱلْأَرْضِ ۚ فَلَا تَأْسَ عَلَى ٱلْقَوْمِ ٱلْفَٰسِقِينَ (٢٦)

(Their Lord) said: For this the land will surely be forbidden them for forty years that they will wander in the earth, bewildered. So, grieve not over the wrongdoing folk. (26)

This verse has fourteen words in Arabic, which reflects half the days of one month. Adding 14 with 26, which is the number of the verse, the sum is 40. It describes the forty years that Israeli people wandered the earth when they refused entry to the holy land. I am not here to discuss the story itself, but the relationship between the numbers and how they align.

On the page containing this verse, there are three mentions of Allah, each with four letters in Arabic, for a total of twelve. There are also three Lords (*Rabbi*). If totaled, they are seven. Twelve and seven are time-related numbers. The verse describes forty years. Adding 26 and 14 is 40. Why is the structure of the verses in the Quran often related to the numbers they contain?

The miracle is that the highlighted part contains forty letters in Arabic!

I accept the greatness of the One who invented the Quran. It came from someone with knowledge of mathematics far beyond humans in the seventh century.

THE NUMBER 13

In Islam, there are no unlucky numbers. In the early 1980s, certain unlucky numbers were introduced to our society from other Western cultures, like the number thirteen.

I reviewed several cultures but didn't find any complications with the number thirteen, other than American culture, which focuses on Friday the thirteenth—although the USA flag has thirteen strips. In Italy, thirteen is a lucky number, and Jewish boys are considered mature on their thirteenth birthday. In the last supper of Jesus, there were thirteen people, and Shi›a Muslims have thirteen imams.

In the Quran, many verses contain the number thirteen. This aligns with concepts of time, although I only examine certain examples. Let's look at the pages in the Quran containing the number thirteen and see how they interact with the time.

Table 5

Page No.	# of Allah
13	2
113	3
213	6
313	1
413	13
513	9
Total	**34**

The numerical and time correlations in the Quran

If we multiply all the number of times Allah is mentioned on each page, we get 4,212.

If we separate the numbers, we get twelve and forty-two. The twelve represents the hours in a day or night. If we divide 4212 by the number of times Allah is mentioned in surah *Al-Tawbah*, we get 23.93.

$4212/176 = 23.93$ hours, or ~24

If we divide 4212 by the number of hours in a day or night (12 hrs), we get 351.

$4212/12 = 351$

If we count the words that are used to refer to Allah without directly naming him, we get seven in total. If we divide seven by the number of times the word رَبّ appears, which is two, we get 3.5. Now, if we add that to our previous calculation we get 354.5, reflecting the lunar year.

$7/2 = 3.5$
$351 + 3.5 = 354.5$

Finally, the notorious number 169 in *Al-Tawbah* is thirteen squared.

$\sqrt{169} = 13$
Or $13 \times 13 = 169$

INHERITANCE

In the Quran, there are many verses regulating how relatives inherit from each other when somebody in the family passes away. The amazing thing is that all the ratios are time-related numbers.

In surah *An-Nissa*, the ratios have a common denominator. They are 1/2, 1/3, 1/4, 1/6, 1/8, and 2/3. The common denominator of all the fractions is twenty-four, reflecting the hours of a full day.

****

The numbers in most verses describe something related to time. In the following tables, I demonstrate how the verses that carry numbers provide time-related numbers when added subtracted, multiplied, or grouped.

Note that most of the selected verses describe something directly or indirectly related to time. I selected certain surahs as an example to demonstrate how the Quran's verses are mathematically coded with time.

Table 6

Al-Baqarah

Verse number	Result	Relation/contents
43 (4 x 3)	12	Prayer/zakat
56 (5x6)	30	Death
65 (6x5)	30	Saturday
83 (8x3)	24	Zakat/Salat
146 (1x4x6)	24	Prophet Muhammad
174 (1+7+4)	12	Day
212 (2 x 12)	24	Day
226 (2x6) x2	24	Months
228 (2+2+8)	12	Day and months
234 (2x3x4)	24	Months
238 (2x3x8)	48	Salat
240 (24+0)	24	Year
258 (2+5+8)	15	Life, death, and the sun
260 (2x6) +0	12	Life, death
264 (2+6+4)	12	Day
274 (27+4)	31	Day, night
282 (2+8+2) The longest verse	12	Life span

Table 7

Al-Imran

Verse number	Result	Relation/contents
59 (5+9)	14	Jesus creation
$49\sqrt{49}$	7	Death, life, creation
72 (7x2)	14	Day, night
106 (1+0+6)	7	Day
113 (1+13)	14	Night
140 (14+0)	14	Days
143 (1x4x3)	12	Death
$144\sqrt{144}$	12	Death of Muhammad
156 (1x5x6)	30	Death, life
185 (1+8+5)	14	Death, life, day
194 (1+9+4)	14	Day

Table 8

An-Nissa

Verse number	Result	Relation/contents
15	15	Death
29	29	Death
39 (3+9)	12	Day

The numerical and time correlations in the Quran

43 (4x3)	12	Salat
87 (8+7)	15	Day
93 (9+3)	12	Death
102 (10+2)	12	Salat
159 (1+5+9)	15	Day, death

****

There are many verses related to time, but I selected the simplest and easiest to interpret to make it easier for the reader. This is only beginning of new era of studying the Quran to test it mathematically and statistically. Perhaps the next step is to use highly sophisticated machines to investigate how words, letters, and numbers in the Quran have related each other. We may find that this investigation raises more questions than answers.

What makes the Quran impressive is not its historical authenticity but how it correlates numerically and mathematically to numerous scientific phenomena. In this probe, I have not considered the historical aspects of the text, but instead investigated how the Quran is related to concepts of time. I believe that God is communicating with us through the messengers who revealed Quran.

If Allah writes about a specific topic, is He aware that His words are harmonized with it mathematically? For instance, I looked with curiosity at verses that mention day, night, months, the sun, the moon, surahs, and others that had time-related numbers. What I discovered was stunning. With more time and technological tools, I would prove further that that this book is not the work of a human, but of divine origin.

27 Ramadan, 1439 H
11 June 2018 AD
Seattle, Washington
United States of America

Printed in Canada